T0267352

Praise for *Embracing Queer Family*

"*Family* is a contested term for LGBTQIA+ persons, and family is essential to feel normal again. Finding the right kinds of familial ties or relationships, whether biological or chosen, is essential for Queer people and Queer families. Bonds of love are what help reduce harm against those of us who are different. This book shows us the way of one family's journey toward normalcy and building Queer family. I hope you will read it and learn, as I have learned, how essential feeling normal is for Queer and Transgender folks."

—**Roberto Che Espinoza**, PhD, author of *Activist Theology* and *Body Becoming: A Path to Our Liberation*

"In *Embracing Queer Family*, Nia and Katie have written a deeply compassionate and helpful guide for Queer and trans folks and the people who love them. They encourage understanding, differentiation, and loving boundaries—all of which are necessary for strong relationships—and provide a beautiful illustration of the truth that freedom for one person can lead to freedom for others as well. The included questions for reflection and examples of helpful phrases for conversation make this a must-have book for those navigating the early stages of coming out and inviting in."

—**Austen Hartke**, author of *Transforming: The Bible and the Lives of Transgender Christians*

"This tender, insightful, and substantive book will help you, your family, and your community respond with love to a Queer family member. Drawing from the authors' own experience, it helps you navigate through confusion and conflict to trust, hope, and love."

—**Brian D. McLaren**, author of *Faith After Doubt*

"I've been Queered in my relationships to friends, family, and congregants. Though I am cis and straight, my theology has been Queered. I see God differently, preach differently, advocate more passionately for a world in which my queer and becoming beloveds *know* for sure they are magical and created in the image of God. Nia and Katie have Queered me, with beautiful work, stories, anecdotes, wisdom, frank and fierce love. Get ready, you will be Queered too. A must-read! Thank you, Nia and Katie!"

—**Rev. Dr. Jacqui Lewis**, senior minister for Public Theology and Transformation at Middle Church; author of *Ten Essential Strategies for Becoming a Multiracial Congregation* and *The Power of Stories*

"We all deserve to find a little peace for ourselves, and Katie and Nia help us to discover ourselves most gently with this book. They also remind us that while our stories are not the same, we can see ourselves in each other and our collective power as Queer folks."

—**Courtney Reyes**, LGBTQ+ advocate

Embracing
Queer Family

embracing queer family

Learning *to* Live Authentically *in* Our Families *and* Communities

NIA CHIARAMONTE *and* KATIE J. CHIARAMONTE

Broadleaf Books
Minneapolis

‘

EMBRACING QUEER FAMILY
Learning to Live Authentically in Our Families and Communities

Library of Congress Control Number: 2023025894 (print)

Cover design: john calmeyer
Cover image: alexander-grey-jYbKxinWQGk-unsplash.jpg/GettyImages-1418723773.jpg

Print ISBN: 978-1-5064-9086-1
eBook ISBN: 978-1-5064-9092-2

Printed in China.

To our children, who have taught us what love looks like and the beauty of embracing ourselves exactly as we are.

And to those who have been with us on this journey, we could never have travelled these roads without you.

CONTENTS

INTRODUCTION

"I just want to feel normal again."

Katie's words landed on the table in front of us like a load of bricks. We were enjoying one of our first dinners out together as wives at a sweet New Mexican restaurant in Albuquerque, far away from our Iowa home. Nia had come out to Katie in July 2018 as a transgender woman after fourteen years of marriage, and we had held her identity in privacy until this moment in late March 2019. We had come to Albuquerque for a conference on contemplative spirituality spearheaded by Richard Rohr and thought that this was as good a time as any for Nia to live her gender identity full time. We found out we were correct after diligently searching for a safe bathroom in the convention center. Come to find out the conference had marked off gender-neutral bathrooms specifically for transgender and nonbinary people. We could breathe a little.

Being out in this place had opened up the possibility for Nia that living this way, as an out, transgender woman, could be feasible full time. As we ventured out to dinner that night, it seemed obvious that things were about to change. After holding Nia's transgender identity in privacy for nearly two years as a couple, it seemed to Katie as if *normal* was never going to be our reality again. We'd seen many unexpected life events within our marriage, so change wasn't foreign to us. However, the idea of shifting our lives from a straight-facing couple in our religiously and socially conservative corner of the world to living our truth as we knew it seemed nearly impossible.

For Katie, wanting to be "normal again" was her expression of her acceptance of Nia's identity and what it meant for us, of wanting to move toward a new reality so we could normalize it. The room to breathe in New Mexico was ushering in a sense of hope for what was possible. But Nia heard "normal again" and internalized it. In her fear of losing our family and all we had built together, she understood Katie's comment as a declaration that she couldn't keep walking this journey toward transition. Understanding the reality that Katie was expressing her willingness to move forward felt too out of reach, too hopeful. But Nia realized that going backward, living as a man, was not possible for her. She knew that returning to the old definition of *normal* wasn't an option. She felt trapped in an untenable position between a wife and family that she loved and the truth of herself that she couldn't keep hidden anymore.

That word, *normal*, reverberated in both of our ears throughout the remainder of our dinner and on arriving back at our rented casita, there was no denying we were at a turning point. Nia expressed her distress at the idea of remaining in a box she felt may quite literally kill her. Katie watched as Nia melted into a deep despair and held her as she processed through her need for freedom, reassuring her that her need for normalcy didn't mean a regression but an acceptance, a moving forward.

Something broke that night. In all of the most devastating and beautiful ways. As Nia released the former male version of herself, she broke through a barrier and began to inhale sweet, fresh air. Katie watched as Nia took her first breath in her new life, and a wave of relief swept through them both. Katie realized that she, too, had been holding the air in her lungs, and as she exhaled all of her resistance, it was replaced by the fresh breeze of hope. We had learned to breathe with new breath, but now we were in the liminal space, uncertain of what was to come.

Welcome, friend. Take a deep breath. Let down your shoulders. Unclench your jaw. We know that whatever has brought you to this book, it is likely you are carrying a heavy weight inside you. Whether you are a Queer[1] individual on the journey of self-awareness, an ally looking for resources, or a family member seeking advice on how to navigate a loved one's coming-out process, this book is for you. You may feel incredibly excited about your journey, confused about what you are experiencing, supportive of friends and family, or even frustrated and defiant over the place you find yourself. This is the liminal space, the space between what was and what will be, and you may be uncertain of what comes next. We understand, and there is room for it all. Here in these pages, you will not find judgment or coercion. We hope you will find space to expand, to question, and to get comfortable not having the answers. We want you to know that no one walks this road perfectly, but that doesn't mean you have to walk it alone. We can walk it together in love.

Every individual has a unique personal journey to their gender and sexual identity. For some, understanding these facets of our identity is something that comes easily and early. For others, self-awareness is hard-fought and comes later in life. For all of us, our awareness of who we are continues to grow, develop, and evolve over time. Our openness to this evolution and the way in which we approach new challenges can help us move through our life stages with more grace, empathy, and love. We all bring our special perspective to life's various changing landscapes, and the more we know about ourselves, the easier it is to make room for one another.

Just like you, we come to this book with our own distinct experiences. We recognize that our story may not look like your story, and it's unlikely our circumstances will match yours. We think this is a good thing. It's time we stop loading all LGBTQIA+ experiences into the same basket, both in our own minds and in the narratives we tell society. Honoring the reality that no two people find themselves in the exact same way is a great first step in understanding and trusting each other. Queer or not, respect starts when we set aside our preconceptions and the notion that we know or understand someone better than they know or understand themselves.

If we, Nia and Katie, believed that who we are on the surface is all we are, we never would have found ourselves or the beauty and depth of love we now share. We don't have to hide, consciously or not, parts of who we are. We grew up together in an environment of strong religious conviction that had strict roles for men and women and incredibly stringent purity standards. These rules gave us guidelines for life that, on the one hand, fostered a communal sense of morality and stability and, on the other, prevented us from exploring the depths of our gender and sexuality. We adhered rigidly to our faith's dogma and rules as a way to satiate the guilt and anxiety that grew inside of us for reasons we didn't quite understand.

We were lucky enough to find each other in our small private school and became best friends in middle school, a couple in high school, and then married in college at the age of twenty-one. We both saved our first sexual experiences for marriage, and

Nia is the only person Katie has ever kissed. In our minds and the minds of those in our community, we had made it! We were a straight-facing couple who followed the letter of the law and were blessed with a loving marriage full of great sexual experiences and tender love for one another.

Our family grew quickly from one child to three children in four years, and soon after we added another child to our family through adoption. We lived a rigorous life of family, friends, and faith. We were, by all accounts, happy people with a beautiful family. Yet both of us were suffering, trying to work out the ache that lived deep inside of us, unaware that the other was struggling.

Our internal journeys were about to spill onto the surface of our lives. Throughout the book, we will dive deeper into the nuances of our story, but for the moment, let us summarize as best we can to get us all on the same page.

Katie, who had always lived with intense anxiety that had turned into a deep depression during college, was now experiencing inexplicable pain and weight loss that doctors diagnosed as fibromyalgia. After visiting a homeopath, she discovered that her cortisol levels—the hormone associated with stress—were through the roof and were starting to affect her bodily functions. Meanwhile, Nia was also struggling with a secret shame that reared its head in times of stress and anxiety. A cycle of secret female gender expression followed by intense shame was building up and threatening to make itself known. In the midst of all of this, we became pregnant with our fifth baby and moved to a rural area just outside of our midwestern city to try to find some peace.

In order to become healthy, we had to get help, and that started with each other. Through a series of events that included long conversations and extensive therapy, Nia was able to come out to Katie as a transgender woman. Through Nia's own coming-out process, Katie was gifted the opportunity to explore her gender and sexuality, finding parts of herself she had never been able to name before, and eventually came out as Queer. Together, we have been able to wrestle with the shame and guilt that have plagued us and have been able to support each other as we find the beauty of who we are. The road to self-awareness has been difficult and painful, but we are standing together with pride in who we are and the family that we have built.

In September 2022, on Nia's fortieth birthday, we stood before friends and family and renewed our vows to one another. After eighteen years of marriage, we find ourselves in a place we'd never imagined. Our five children are thriving and happy. Our marriage is strong and life-giving. We are making moves that satisfy our deep longings. We are living out lifelong dreams, like writing a book together and moving across the country to the East Coast after forty years in Iowa. Had we closed ourselves off to the rich truth of ourselves and each other, we wouldn't be where we are today. It has taken work and has been full of every emotion, but finding ourselves and each other has been the most fruitful, loving work of our lives.

We want to invite you into this kind of labor that allows us all to be fully ourselves while embracing those around us. For those of us who are Queer, this looks like inviting others into our journey and trusting them to hold and support us. As family and friends of Queer individuals, our work is to listen to and trust our loved ones while exploring our own reactions and seeking to understand ourselves more deeply. This is truly a labor of love that yields unexpected crops of joy and safety. For some of our loved ones, the ability to love and support us comes easily. Like

INTRODUCTION

it did for Katie's younger sister and Nia's best friend, who had already done much of their own work surrounding their inclusion of Queer folks in their lives. Those who have been laying the groundwork to know themselves are often ready to step in and tend the garden of souls searching for ourselves.

For others, joining in the labor may mean a cracking open of the blossom of their own identity. Like flowers unfurling together in the spring, those who are searching for themselves often find the strength to bloom in numbers. Still others may find this work dreadful, even impossible. It may seem selfish and even sinful for those who haven't had the opportunity to take part in this kind of work before or who have been taught a deep-seated homophobia through their religious or cultural contexts. It may be loathsome work that they fight every step of the way. To those feeling this way, we say, congratulations—you are here. You are doing the hard work toward understanding. If you have even made it this far into this book, you are five steps ahead of many people who feel the pressure of shame and judgment and choose not to enter into the work of lovingly embracing Queer family. Thank you for reading. Please know that you are important to the healthy development of those you love, and they are important to yours. Together, we mold each other.

We must also acknowledge that there will be those who cannot do this work, whether due to conviction, coercion, or simply because they are unwilling to put themselves through the pain of this labor. Some of those who we love are not able to dig in and uncover new depths of life and love with us. While this is painful and can also be traumatic, we want you to know that it is okay. It is their choice, and if we are to be true to ourselves, we must allow others to be true to themselves. No one should be forced into this work. It is each person's individual choice how far they are willing to go to understand the other. We will discuss more on this topic later in the section on boundaries, but for now, we hope we can sit with you in the grief of knowing that not everyone is ready or willing. That has nothing to do with who you are. It is their choice. You are worth loving well, and there are many people in this world waiting for you with open arms.

While our story is unique, we have learned many things from others who are in the coming-out process. Our backgrounds in family studies, psychology, and spirituality have also helped us navigate and engage in the hard work of knowing ourselves. What we have learned is that no one can do this alone. The work of becoming takes support, tension, questioning, and, above all, trusted loved ones to walk alongside us.

During our process of coming out, Katie became a birth doula and immediately began to connect the dots between the physical birthing process and the process of birthing our identities into the world. Simply put, a birth doula is someone who holds the space for a birthing person, provides emotional support, and lends empathy and encouragement. By definition, doulas cannot do the job of the birthing person. We can only stand as a loving witness to the process, reminding the one in labor that they are not alone, that the pain they are feeling is natural, and holding them as they release a new soul into the world.

We would like to offer ourselves as this kind of companion to you. We desire to sit beside you on your journey to self-discovery and all that entails. Whether you are the central figure in this story or you are playing a supporting role, everyone needs a doula. Birth doulas are not often someone inside the birthing person's family. We need space and emotional distance in order to see clearly and without making the narrative about ourselves. We had several beautiful doulas on our journey who sat with us in difficult conversations and held us through our darkest nights. These people have become some of our dearest friends, but at the outset, they had the objectivity we needed to help us without owning what was happening as theirs. We are eternally grateful for these beloved human beings.

We do not claim to know or understand everyone's experience, and we view this as another good thing. As we move together through the coming pages, we hope that our words will breathe and move for you and that you will interact with them, push back, and enter into the conversation. Our experiences are just that—ours. We have learned which steps and movements were most helpful to us as we worked to find ourselves. We are listening closely to others around us to find the signposts present on the road and the tools that illuminate the path. We hope this conversation grows and evolves far beyond us. For now, we offer ourselves as ones who have gone before and will hold you as you birth your becoming into the world.

1

Identity and Support for the Journey

Identity is an intensely personal journey made up of many different facets, including our gender and sexuality. However, none of us holds our identity in a vacuum. Our familial and communal identities are formed by individuals who all bring their own identities to the mix. Our structures of being—our families, our faith communities, our schools, our workplaces—are all systems composed of individuals who inform the group identity; in return, these cultures breathe back into us, helping to inform our own sense of self.

This book breaks down identity into three fundamental parts: individual, family, and community. Each section will build on the last in concentric circles that weave in and out of each other, much like an ancient labyrinth, with the identity of the Queer person set in the middle. We are centering the Queer individual not because other stories do not matter but rather because Queer identity is so infrequently centered and often misunderstood. In addition, if you have found yourself reading this book, it is likely you are looking for guidance, either for your own Queer identity or to better understand how your identity intersects with that of a Queer loved one.

The foundational structure of this book is built on the ring theory of support, developed by Susan Silk and Barry Goldman.[1] Ring theory is essentially a framework for crisis and grief care inside of community. The theory suggests that we live our lives in a structure made up of concentric circles that create our communal experiences. When we come under stress, we should be centered inside of that structure that acts almost as a ripple. Those providing the most support or who are closest in proximity to us and our journey make up the inner rings. Those with less proximity and closeness reside in the outer. The theory suggests this centering can compound care and diffuse stress if our supportive allies give us safety through our period of stress, allowing us to walk through it in a way that is true to ourselves and ultimately healing, while managing their own emotions with others further afield of the situation.

What we love about ring theory is that it addresses the many entities contributing to an individual's journey. Silk and Goldman used this framework for care through crisis, and we think it applies to care through the discovery of identity, which for some comes as a crisis and for others comes as a relief. We would like to reframe ring theory's foundation of support through crisis into support through change. This allows us all to take off the value judgments associated with our personal reactions to the coming-out journey and simply see ourselves as part of an ever-evolving communal system that is seeking to breathe in synchronicity without strangling any of its members.

As we apply ring theory to the work we're doing in this book, we will also place the individual experiencing the greatest crisis—or, in our case, the greatest change—at the center point.

For our purposes, we are centering the Queer individual and their journey as they are experiencing the greatest level of change and assuming the highest level of risk, something we will address further in the coming chapters. This center point lies within a larger circle we are naming *family*. Family, here, is the system of relationship that you find yourself most closely associated with. For many, *family* is our nuclear families of origin. For others, *family* may include a much broader definition than blood or law relations. We will discuss this further in the "Family" section.

Family is then encircled by an even larger sphere we are naming *community*. Here again, your personal definition of community will become important. Throughout this book, we will walk you through determining who is a part of your community, who is affected by this change, and who is in and out of your system of support. Here is a visual representation of ring theory structure for easy reference:

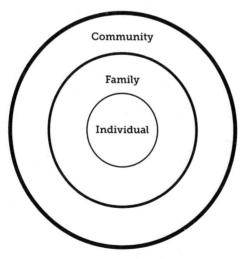

Figure 1: Ring Theory Structure

We will refer back to this structure often as we find it is one of the most important building blocks for understanding our personal identities and how we affect one another as we move and grow. We find it crucial to identify what each of these spheres looks like and who is allowed into which arena of our life. This work may require that strong lines or boundaries be drawn between each of these circles and even around individuals who inhabit these circles. This is not to distance us from one another; rather, it serves to differentiate us from one another. A large part of the work we are embarking on is understanding where *I* end and *you* begin, what I am responsible for and what you are responsible for, and how our actions and reactions affect one another as individual human beings.

Another essential factor in ring theory is the idea that support moves inward and "dumping," or emotional release, flows outward, like this:

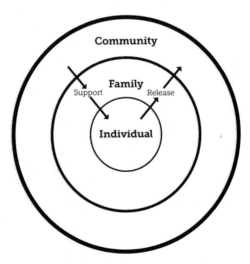

Figure 2: Flow of Support and Release

Every person who makes up these circles will inevitably need support and also release during the process of understanding one another more fully. Ring theory reminds us that as emotions and support move inward, they compound, and as they move outward, they disperse. When support flows inward, it compounds, allowing the person experiencing greater levels of change to be bolstered by the love and encouragement of others. Loving support helps to widen the lens that allows us to see ourselves and one another fully without shame. When we are allowed to shake off shame, we are able to more accurately navigate ourselves without the need to dig in our heels or give up ourselves inappropriately.

Conversely, if we're not the individual in the center, when we feel difficult emotions, the tendency can be to turn inward and cast blame. Ring theory reminds us to own our feelings and seek support from those who are not experiencing feelings as intensely or closely, so we do not crush those in the inner circles with the weight of our emotions. This is important because it allows us to seek loving care from those we have identified as part of our circles of support in our family and community without fear of being castigated, shamed, or manipulated. In addition, those whom we trust who are further removed from immediate change are likely to come with clearer heads—especially those who have dedicated themselves to loving us well through the changes we are facing. This is why deciding who will be a part of our circles is vitally important.

As we begin our journey together, we invite you to begin to think about who falls into your circles of support within your community and family and where they belong. Take time to think about who is closest to you and may be most affected as well as who may be able to provide the most emotional safety for you. It is also important to think about those who are more removed from your journey but may be able to provide support. We find it helpful to also identify those in your circles who may not be as supportive while still keeping an open mind. People surprise us all the time. At the outset, you may have more difficulty placing people into the correct circles or finding a place for them at all. As we move throughout the pages of this book, you may find that some people change circles, and some may need to move beyond these inner circles to outer ones that you get to define. When we know more about ourselves, it becomes easier to see who belongs in our community and our circles of support.

When we began our journey of transition, our circles looked a lot different. We were disappointed in many ways, but overwhelmingly, we have been joyfully surprised by those who have become residents in our community and family circles. It's also true that these circles are ever-changing and evolving. Sometimes stricter boundaries are needed when there is a particularly tough issue. Often, though, and more with time, we find our walls are becoming more and more porous, allowing for more growth in our circles. It is absolutely okay if your circles shrink before they widen. It's all part of the process.

At the end of each section, we will provide reflections, exercises, and rituals to help set up guideposts for our journey together. Please revisit these often and share them with those you love. Doing these exercises together or sharing your insights may also help bridge gaps in understanding and bring you closer together.

As we move forward, we encourage you to fill out your own circles of support. Take your time as some people will be easily identified and others may need a little more time. You don't have to think about who *should* be a part of the circles but rather who you *want* to be a part of them. It may be helpful to start with something like Brené Brown's "Square Squad" activity to identify your innermost circle first.[2] For this activity, you cut a one-inch-by-one-inch piece of paper and write down the people—only as many as can fit in the square—whose opinions matter to you. As you move forward, you can return to this list and to these circles to remember who matters most to you in your life. Sometimes, people who start on that small list will need to be removed. Reminder: this is support, and those involved in your circles should be those who are ready and willing to love you fiercely without guilt or shame. It's time to find your team. This is where it all begins.

Reflection

Circles of Support Worksheet

Use the diagram and questions below to think about your circles of support:

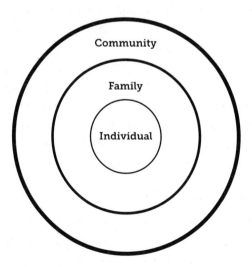

Figure 1: Ring Theory Structure

Who Is the Individual in the Center?

* If this is me, how do I need support?
* If this is a loved one, how do I need to support them?
* If this is a loved one, how do I need support? Look for this from the outer circle, not from the individual in the center.

Who Is in the Family Circle?

For each member of this circle, think about the following:

* Is this family member in the circle of support, or do they need another boundary for the time being? We will discuss this in later chapters.
* What kind of support can this family member bring?
* What kind of support may this family member need?
* If I am not a part of this family circle, how can I support the family?
* If I am a part of the family circle, how can I support the other members of the family circle without emotionally dumping on them?
* If I am a part of the family circle, what resistance might I feel, and where can I find loving support as I process?
* Within the family circle, what are the other levels of support surrounding individuals? For instance, the spouse or parent of the Queer individual needs to be the nexus of their own circle of support.

Who Is in the Community Circle?

* Who or what makes up my community?
* Are there community members who may be more supportive than others? Who are they?

* What kind of support does my community bring?
* What kind of resistance might my community bring?
* Is this community safe for me?
* If I am a member of this community, how do I feel about this change?
* If I am a member of this community, can I support this change?
* If I am a member of this community, how can I process my resistance if I have any?

For All Members of the Circle

* How committed am I to the well-being of the individual in the center?
* Am I able to trust the levels of support and release?
* What will be my reminder to myself to honor the circles of support?

2

Introduction of Terms
and Landmarks

Language is very important, especially in the case of our identities, so we want to be clear about the terms we are using and the landmarks we will be pointing out along the way. All individuals come to any given situation with their own set of preconceptions about what words mean and how they are used. In order to streamline conversation, we'd like to start out together. As we are about to move through our journey, we will be discussing several terms and significant landmarks that deserve a little extra attention before we embark. Even if you believe you know the meanings of these words, please take time to familiarize yourself with the way we are using them here in order to provide an even starting place for us all.

Identity

Throughout this book, we will be using the word *identity* liberally. We will be specifically speaking about identity as it pertains to gender and sexuality. However, we also want to address the larger concept of identity and how we can, so often, confuse our identity with our ideology and practice. It is important to know the distinction between who we are, what we think about who we are, and how we interact with ourselves and others based on these factors.

Identity, as we will refer to it, is who we know ourselves to be at our core. This is something no one else can tell us about ourselves. Identity is not always known to us, but it is always there for us to discover. There are many psychological and spiritual ways to define identity that are worthy of exploration. However, we find the simplest way to understand our identities is to think of things we cannot take off. For example, for years, Nia "put on" a male identity to allow herself to move safely inside of a world that would have rejected the person whom she knew herself to be. She was so adept at living inside of this armor that she repressed parts of herself for years, but she was never able to completely overcome the feeling that she was indeed female. Everything on the outside screamed *male*, but deep inside herself, Nia knew this was not who she truly is. Until she stopped fighting her identity, she always felt as if a piece of herself was missing. When she was able to remove her armor of manhood, she was finally able to see herself as who she knew she had always been.

When we fight against our identity, we end up betraying the very parts of ourselves that make us who we are. Gender and sexuality are just two facets of our identities. However, they are a large part of who we are. Some identities are innate—things we are born with—and some evolve over time. Each part of our identity makes up the specificity of who we are as a person and affects how we experience the world. As we grow, we begin to form ideas and opinions about ourselves and others; this is what we call *ideology*.

We find that people often confuse ideology with identity, believing that the way they think or believe about something or someone is who they are at their core. Ideology is how we frame the world so that it makes sense to us. It is what we believe, how we think, and the dogmas we adhere to based on our ability to reason through our experience of the world. Many of us inherit these ideologies from a lineage of cultural or religious practices that inform how we see the world. While it feels as though our ideology is our identity, it is in fact something that is malleable and flexible when we are presented with new experiences and information. A good example of this is the myriad denominations or sects of a religion. Our religious identity may be Christian, but the denominational ideology of a fundamentalist Southern Baptist is very different from that of a progressive Episcopalian. Both identify as Christian, but their thoughts, beliefs, and even religious dogmas about their experience of the world are vastly different.

We understand from personal experience that ideology can feel like identity. However, when we take time to explore our beliefs, such as "being Queer is a sin," we may discover that believing this may not be as foundational to our own identity as we once suspected. When we understand the difference between our ideology and our identity, it can be easier to move beyond protecting our thoughts and beliefs to expanding how we interact with others based on a broader and more elemental definition of ourselves.

This will inevitably affect our practice, which is how we interact with ourselves and others based on our individual and social identities. When we are in a protective mode, believing that our identities—which are really our ideologies—are under attack, our practices can become combative at worst and isolating at best. In our need to prove our ideologies, we create division where there doesn't need to be any. If we can understand where our ideologies come from and examine them in the light of our true identities, we are likely to find more commonalities than differences. We can see each other instead of what we think about each other.

It is likely that as you approach this book, you will be bringing ideas about both your identity and your ideologies. For those Queer folks looking to express who they are, we support you in your journey to own your sexual and/or gender identity with pride. For family, friends, and community members struggling to understand your support for your Queer loved ones, we encourage you to examine your beliefs and weigh them against your feelings for the Queer folks in your life. We believe that love is much closer to all of our core identities than hate will ever be. When we don't quite know the answers yet, may our practice be love.

Queer

You may have noticed the use of the word *Queer* already sprinkled throughout these first few pages. We use the word *Queer* as shorthand that has been reclaimed by the LGBTQIA+ community to recognize anyone who does not identify as heterosexual and cisgender. We also want to acknowledge that while we use the *Queer* label for ourselves, not everyone takes this label on with enthusiasm as it has been used to marginalize whole groups of people in the past. Know that while we use it for ourselves, we honor those who don't.

As the LGBTQIA+ umbrella grows, we also acknowledge that Queer identities come to us in ways that don't always fit conventional categories. Katie, for instance, resists labels, but if pressed, she would say she considers herself ambiguously Queer. She knows she isn't strictly straight, but labels such as *bisexual* and *lesbian* don't seem to fit either. In many ways, her Queer identity is still making itself known. This is especially important when we realize that for some, finding a label for their identity has given them a sense of belonging. Katie works hard to not claim Queerness in a way that doesn't fit for her and, in that respect, has chosen an expansive way to identify herself. Nia, on the other hand, came to her Queer identity quickly. When she came out as transgender, she immediately took on the label of *Queer* as it was foundational to identity-building for her.

We understand that for many outside of the LGBTQIA+ community, *Queer* is a difficult word to wrap their minds around. It makes absolute sense that those outside of the Queer community have difficulty understanding the broad use of this word given its history of being weaponized against LGBTQIA+ people. We want to encourage those who find this word difficult to talk to your Queer loved one about the use of this word and its reclamation within the community. For many of us, it is important to not allow those outside of our community to define us but for us to own who we are loud and proud.

For those of us who, like Nia, have found a comfortable label for our Queer identity, we can take this time to speak out loud who we are and engage in conversation with our loved ones about how the word *Queer* helps build our identity. After identifying yourself to your own heart and then to those around you, we freely invite you to exchange *Queer* for your identifying place under the umbrella. While we wish we could outline every aspect of all Queer identities here, that would be a book unto itself! Instead, we encourage you to check out the glossary of terms on PFLAG's website, www.pflag.org/glossary. It is an incredibly detailed list that can help you gain insight into yourself and/or your loved ones.

It is also important to note that our identities are not always static. As our awareness of ourselves grows, we may feel like one label or another fits us better. This is why we appreciate the roominess of the word *Queer*. It allows us to evolve as people and invites us to think more expansively about who we are. Without the wide-open invitation of the term *Queer*, many of us may never find ourselves as knowing ourselves is difficult without context. Our values, beliefs, emotions, and experiences all shape us. As we grow, we may find that we become more fluid. This is exactly what *Queer* embodies. There's no reason to choose one or another label if it doesn't fit. *Queer* invites us into the world of both/and, not either/or. It allows us to know ourselves *and* explore ourselves at the same time.

As the spectrum of Queer identities grows, we hope that the support within this book can expand as well. By allowing the inclusiveness of the word *Queer* to lead the way, we commit ourselves to loving the whole Queer family and embracing each other with dignity and respect.

Letting In

One landmark on our journey in each of the three circles of identity will be that of *letting in*. This is a term we have used in our own private lives to distinguish between bringing others into our process of identity formation versus coming out publicly, which we will talk about next. The definitive trait of letting in is that it is a private revealing of oneself to another with the intention of entering into a supportive relationship as we explore our identity. Often, letting in happens before we are completely sure what our identities mean to us or which actions we will take. It is important that letting in happens with people whom we trust, who are safe, and who will not try to control our identity formation.

Letting in is an incredibly vulnerable action that involves a great deal of both real and perceived risk on the part of the person disclosing their identity. When the time came for Nia to let Katie in on who she is as a transgender woman, the moment was full of fear and trepidation. How would Katie respond? What if this was the end of our marriage? What does being transgender even mean? Although Nia didn't have all the answers, she knew that she could not continue to uncover more about her identity without this letting in. Letting in, although done in a relationship that is perceived to be safe, doesn't come without risks. In this case, Nia invited Katie into her process of self-discovery at great risk to their relationship, marriage, and family life. Her courage in vulnerability allowed her to become a truer version of herself and allowed Katie to love her more fully.

NIA LEAN-IN: Coming out to Katie was the hardest thing I've done in my life. As much as I was confident I'd be met with a loving response, I was less sure where this left our relationship, our marriage, and our family.

I had spent months of therapy searching for my identity, and when I stumbled across it suddenly in a session one morning—the label of *transgender* sitting inside my soul like it had been there all along—I knew I had to tell Katie. We had been together for eighteen years and married for fourteen of those years. I knew this was not something I could sit on for any length of time. I did, however, want to have the conversation in person.

On my way home from work that day, I planned how I would tell her that I was transgender. I ran through many scenarios but settled on feeling her out. I would hedge my bets. I'd say something like, "So what do you think about trans people? I might be trans. What do you think about that?" If she reacted poorly, I'd back off, saying something like, "I mean, maybe I'm trans but probably not."

But thanks to the long drive, as I reflected further, I knew this wasn't fair. It wasn't fair to the woman whom I had grown to love so dearly over many years to withhold my honesty. It wasn't fair to start a new chapter, a new dynamic between us, with a half-truth. So I changed my mind. I would tell her straight away.

The rest of that night was a blur. I'm sure we had dinner; I'm sure we watched a show as a family and put the kids to bed as usual, but I don't remember any of it. My heart thumping the whole time, I waited for the moment when we were alone and I was able to say to her, "I need to tell you something." Always the scariest way to start a conversation for the person on the receiving end for sure, but I did need to tell her this. I dispensed with the pleasantries, the hedging, and any other delay tactics my brain might have come up with in the moment and just blurted out, "I'm transgender."

The words hung in the air. It seemed as though uncovering my identity and saying it out loud for the first time in such a loaded situation had literally stopped time. It seemed like an hour, but within one second, she responded with a simple "I know."

I make jokes about this now, asking her why she didn't tell me if she knew all along! But in reality, these words were such a beautiful response from a person with whom I had built a life. I knew in that moment that our story would morph and change. I wasn't sure whether we'd stay married in the end, but either way, I knew I was loved. And I think that's what most of us who share our identities with our loved ones really hope for.

As a loved one being let into someone's journey, our job is to listen and hold what we are receiving with tenderness and care. This requires us to put aside our initial feelings and thoughts and allow our Queer loved one to be the center of the story. And that is extremely difficult to do! When Katie was let into Nia's identity, it felt like a bomb had gone off. Then, as Katie listened with mindfulness and love, the feeling of explosion turned to an implosion, reversing the shattering effect of the initial disclosure and shifting pieces of our life together into place. Suddenly, so many things made sense that had plagued Katie's thoughts. She had always felt as though Nia could love her fully, but there was always just a hair's breadth of distance between her love for Nia and what Nia could accept. When Nia let Katie in, Katie was allowed to know Nia in her fullness and therefore to love her more closely than ever before. This was the feeling that Katie held on to when things got confusing and difficult—knowing someone fully allows us to love them fully. Letting in is an enormous gift if we are willing to walk through the door and into the heart of our loved one.

Letting in is not just a step for Queer individuals. It is also a step that family members must take as they navigate this journey with their loved ones. When the time is right, and Queer individuals come out, family members may feel the need to take it slowly as we let others into our circles of support who may not know our Queer loved one's identity. It is vitally important that families discuss the letting-in process and to whom disclosures are to be made. It is a deep betrayal to take someone's identity and disclose it to a third party without that person's knowledge. Whom and when to let in is a decision made in relationship, guided by our Queer loved one's sense of safety and need to come out. The decision of whom to let in is not anyone's but our Queer loved ones, and we should always defer to them.

When Nia was on her journey, she and Katie were holding her identity mostly between the two of them. Nia had online friends whom she could chat with, but Katie was living in a world where it was important to the security of our relationships at the time that Nia's disclosure remained private. When Katie was finally able to let a friend in on her own journey and disclose Nia's identity, with Nia's consent, the weight of all she had been carrying began to dissipate. Then as Katie's sister was let in, a system of support began to form that allowed Katie to be held as she held Nia, and together we could focus on more than the elephant of identity in the room. We now had allies who would be vital to our emotional and spiritual well-being during Nia's coming-out process.

It is important to identify people early on who will be receptive to your letting in. We highly recommend that these are people with whom you feel a great deal of safety and hold respect for. It is also important that these people trust your understanding of your own identity and are able to hold solid boundaries.

Letting in is a scary and beautiful step on the path to deeper understanding, and we will dig into the nitty-gritty more in the coming chapters.

Coming Out

Coming out seems like a very straightforward event. It is usually defined as the public declaration of one's Queer identity. Coming out is a huge milestone in a Queer individual's life. It marks the public commencement of our journey. Now the world gets to see and know us as we see and know ourselves. We can love whom we want without worrying that someone may "find out." We can live as ourselves without hiding any longer. The distinction between *letting in* and *coming out* is that what once was a private conversation among trusted allies is now a public reality for everyone to know. When we let people in, we are asking them into close relationships to lovingly help support us in our identity formation. When we come out, we are saying our identity is not up for discussion.

For some, coming out happens in a big, splashy way—perhaps a post on social media that is met with congratulatory sentiments or even a party. For others, coming out is more subdued, taking place over multiple conversations that let people know "this is who I am, and I want people to know that." Nia had several coming-out experiences because of the different spheres of influence she inhabited and because her disclosure involved a name change, new pronouns, and a completely new presentation to the world. In order to live as herself, Nia had no choice but to be forthcoming and verbal about it.

Katie's coming out was much different. In the early days, it was easier to allow people's assumptions to do their work where her sexuality was concerned. Because of the pace of her own self-exploration, Katie's coming out has been in small doses in one-on-one or small group conversations. Truly, some people who know us and read this book may be surprised to find out Katie identifies as Queer at all! What we have learned is that this is totally okay. Each person gets to handle their coming out their own way. There is no set prescription or "right" way to do it. It simply is, and that's good enough.

One misconception is that we must come out in order to be truly ourselves. We understand that for some people, coming out is not in their plan for any number of reasons. While we encourage the letting in of others to your Queer identity, we realize this isn't always necessary or even desired. Each of us has our own journey. When and if we feel comfortable with coming out is an intensely personal decision worthy of respect.

Another big misconception about coming out is that it only happens once. As we have gotten to know more Queer individuals and have lived this story ourselves, we have come to realize that coming out is a rotating process, kind of like a revolving door. While the initial big *ta-da* moment doesn't always repeat itself, we still have to explain who we are to people again and again. This is especially true for those whose Queer identity is either outwardly obvious like Nia or isn't immediately recognizable like Katie.

Over time, the big buildup of feelings isn't there, but disclosure is still a part of our lives. There are still moments when Katie feels a catch in her throat when she explains her identity to a new doctor or when the parents of our child's friend learn that our family has two moms. Nearly every day, there are moments when Nia has to clarify her gender and/or choose to disclose that she is trans to someone. We take risks on a daily basis to be who we are. We are never *sure* how people will react, but we love ourselves and each other enough to take the risks and let people know who we are.

As we move forward together, we hope you hold these definitions in your mind. If you need to refer back to them, feel free to revisit them at any time. It may also be a good time to discuss with a loved one what these terms mean to you and if you have a different way of interpreting them. These are our definitions for our purposes. However, we know how personal these things can be, and it is important that you understand what they mean for you.

Reflection

Identity

* ✳ How do you feel about the definition of *identity* given above?
* ✳ How do you feel identity and ideology differ?
* ✳ In what ways can you reevaluate your beliefs and/or practice of your ideology to honor others' identities?

Queer

* ✳ What does the word *Queer* mean to me, and how do I feel about its use?
* ✳ What is my gender/sexual identity? Is there a label for it? Does there need to be?
* ✳ How can I engage in conversation about Queer identity?

Letting In

* ✳ If you identify as Queer, can you identify at least one person you can let in to your identity?

* If you haven't let anyone in, what would it feel like to let someone in?
* If you have let someone in, what did that look like? How did it feel? Would you do anything differently?

Coming Out

* If you haven't come out yet, how do you imagine your coming out?
* If your loved one has let you in but hasn't come out yet, what might their coming out look like for you?
* What does coming out mean to you?

3

The Individual Journey In

It seems as though all of us, no matter our gender or sexual identity, are dropped into the middle of a story that is being written around us. Things are moving quickly, and suddenly we realize that the pen is in our hand. While we may have waited for, prayed for, and anticipated being able to take control of our own story, very few of us are ready for it when we are faced with the blank pages of our own lives. Nia was thrust into this moment one summer morning during a therapy session after uttering the words, "I am transgender." All her life, it had felt like something was off, like she had no control over her own story or the world she lived in. Then suddenly with one phrase, the pen was in her hand. Time stood still, and she realized she had a choice. She could let the world around her tell her story, or she could take the pen and write it herself.

Discovering Queer Identity

For many of us, discovering our Queer identity may seem like a monumental task. In fact, we may not even set out to discover our identity, but rather it finds us through our experiences. For some, the discovery of our Queer identity starts during childhood, from as far back as we can remember. Our discovery may have begun in small moments when we were drawn to activities or clothing that are seen as traditionally for the "opposite" gender with the eventual understanding that we are seen as "different" from our peers. It may be a simple declaration as a child that we are a "boy who likes boys" or that we are a girl, even though we have a boy's body.

For others, this discovery takes time. It may take a lot of time. Adults who come to our Queerness over time often have to wade through the mire of shame, societal expectations, and our own understanding of what moving through the world as a Queer person looks like. This task may sometimes come to an abrupt turning point, a sudden realization sparked by a specific event like attending a gay wedding or seeing a trans person on the TV screen. These *a-ha* moments may have been preceded by years of questioning, alongside the feeling that we exist as "other" in society, or may just be the very start of an unfolding journey toward self-understanding.

However, when we begin to see our Queer identities, understanding ourselves more fully can require a lot of self-work. While it's easy to look back after coming to a Queer identity and see all of the signs, in the moment, these things may less obviously be a part of who we are. For many of us, this is because we hold many layers of shame, fear, and stories that we've told ourselves surrounding what it means to be Queer.

Confronting Internalized Queerphobia

Early on in the Queer identity formation process, many of us are confronted with a myriad of emotions. We might be fearful, wondering what this newfound identity means for us or our family. We might have doubts while on the path of self-discovery, second-guessing every identity formation "victory" that comes our way. And for many of us who have religion as a part of our life experience, the overwhelming feeling may be a shame. Even if religion isn't a part of our experience, the shame from societal expectations formed by religion can be thick around us.

While we can't do a deep dive into the anatomy of shame here, we will offer some basic definitions so that we know what we're dealing with. In a 2012 TED Talk, Brené Brown calls shame "the gremlin who says 'never good enough' and . . . 'who do we think we are?'"[1] She also describes the difference between shame and guilt, with guilt being focused on behavior and shame focused on the self. There may be moments of guilt during the identity formation process—I feel bad for the way I treated someone or the way I acted in a situation—but shame typically looms much larger because identity formation is inherently self-focused.

As Queer people, each time we find a piece of ourselves that is counter to the story we have heard before, or maybe even the story we told ourselves about Queer people in our past, we can be flooded with shame. Any negative narrative that we hold about Queerness can turn and point directly at us. For example, in the narrative of "love the sinner, hate the sin"[2] that is often touted in religious circles, we're suddenly the sinner. In the Evangelical Christian faith, which Nia and Katie were a part of for much of our lives, the narrative of human beings as carriers of original sin is only magnified by being Queer. And even without religion directly present in our lives, the message in the public square is that Queer people are "other."

The narrative telling us we're not good enough and that we can't possibly know who we are clouds our ability to continue to build a healthy identity. It's not until we can face this narrative head-on that we can understand its roots and how to stop it from being the primary building blocks for our identities going forward.

For family and friends, watching a loved one turn in on themselves can be very concerning. Shame is one of the foundations that prop up anxiety, depression, and suicidal ideation, and this can be magnified in Queer individuals. In 2022, the Trevor Project released a National Survey on LGBTQ Youth Mental Health revealing that 45 percent of LGBTQ+ youths seriously considered attempting suicide in the past year. They found, however, that the LGBTQ youths who felt high social support from their families reported attempting suicide at less than half the rate of those who felt low or moderate social support. This is the stark difference that love and support for a Queer family member can make to cut through years of shame.[3]

Finding Support before Letting Loved Ones In Therapy

Equally important as a supportive family is finding a good therapist. Many of us are unable to get to a healthy place in our identity without a therapist because of our own unseen corners. These unseen corners have been built up over time, often to protect us from facing something head-on that could have negative results.

For Nia, being Queer wasn't an option. If she had come out as a transgender girl as a child, it would have been unsafe, and naturally her body told her to ignore the possibility entirely. As a child, it was impossible for her to do the work because the unseen corner was built for safety. As an adult, even though her world was somewhat safer for her as a Queer person, that corner remained. There was only so much identity work she could do on her own as she had buried the possibility that she might be transgender so deeply. Only a skilled, licensed therapist could help.

Finding a trusted therapist can also help to build self-trust. Trusting ourselves, our intuition, and our own judgment is often a key step in the journey in. Many of us, especially those of us mired in shame, were taught not to trust ourselves. We may have been told by families, churches, or societal messages that we are bad, so our judgment and understanding about who we are cannot be trusted. Or we simply may not have been taught how to listen to our intuition and our body when they speak to us. Whatever the reason, a good therapist can help guide us out of the fog of self-doubt; past the gremlins that say, "Who do we think we are?" and "We can't possibly know who we are"; and into the fields of self-trust and self-forgiveness.

Finding a trusted therapist, someone who doesn't tell us who we are but guides us with questions on our path to identity formation, is a tall task. For those without insurance to cover the sometimes daily or weekly sessions, it can be even tougher. Fortunately, more and more resources are available for finding a trusted therapist, and more resources for low- and no-cost options can be found in the resource list at the back of this book.[4] We have included this list for easy reference.

Nia found a therapist in her local area who specialized in LGBTQ+ issues. The therapist was gentle and guiding, just what she needed to be able to ask herself the hard questions around gender identity. After a while, though, the questions started to go beyond gender identity into general identity formation. At that point, she found a therapist who specialized in eye movement desensitization and reprocessing (EMDR) therapy and also specialized in LGBTQ+ clients. This therapist came from a referral from a friend, which many times can be the most productive way to find a trusted therapist.

Friends

In addition to possibly referring us to a trusted therapist, friends are a vital part of our support system as we continue the journey in. Having a network of friends who are willing to engage with us where we are and as we are at any given moment is key. For many of us, it can be difficult to find and maintain these deep relationships, especially when we aren't able to live fully authentic lives. We may not be able to be "out" to people or even to ourselves, which can create a barrier to authentic relationships. We'll talk more about letting in those friends who are becoming part of the inner circle later, but before that happens, we have to find friends who will support us in our own growth more generally. This is not to say we have to find friends whom we know are explicitly affirming of Queer identities, as many times we may not even be affirming of our own Queer identity. But we should search for friends who encourage self-growth. Friends who are open to change and growth will be the ones to give us the space to uncover our identities in our most wonderfully whole forms. For both Katie and Nia, this friendship came in the form of one another, and the relationship provided the safety to explore identity along with the encouragement toward growth.

Virtual Friends

While we may not find these growth-minded friends in our social circles, for many of us, the internet has been a safe haven to explore who we are and can even point us quite effectively toward others who may be questioning their identities in the same way. The internet is a powerful tool for connection in the absence of an in-person relationship; however, it is also fraught with potentially damaging conversations as well as individuals who are intent on breaking relationship boundaries around every corner. As we find support online, we have to make sure to protect our identities and our very fragile, growing selves by disengaging with damaging rhetoric and conversation and understanding healthy boundaries. More on this later.

Finding the Right Support System

Landing on the right people and systems to support us as we build identity is a task, to be sure. But we can ask ourselves some specific questions along the way to be sure we're on the right track. First and foremost, do these people/systems that I find myself in and around allow me to be myself in my current state? If yes, good. We're on the right track, but there's more. Some other questions to consider are:

* How do these people/systems feel about me changing and growing?
* Do they encourage curiosity and exploration?
* If I go beyond who I am now or who they think I am, will I be chastised or ostracized?
* If my understanding of my identity grows and changes, will it put me in physical, mental, and/or emotional danger?

Answering these questions can be complex, and oftentimes the answers are not black and white. We may be in a religious system that does not encourage exploration, but our best friend who has our back and supports our growth may be a part of that system as well. We have to weigh the damage that systems or relationships are doing to our journey in, alongside the risk of leaving those same systems or relationships when they are harmful. There are no easy answers.

The journey in is complex. It's difficult, exciting, scary, and exhilarating all at the same time. We take two steps forward, one back, three sideways, and two slantways. The journey is hardly ever a straight line, and our identity-building is influenced by those around us. Hopefully, if we've surrounded ourselves with the right support system and understand the boundaries inside of those relationships and systems, we can make decisions about how to proceed with the support, safety, and insight but not the demands of those systems and relationships.

Owning Our Stories

While finding supportive systems and relationships is key to creating a safe space for ourselves in order to grow, moving forward requires self-differentiation. One of the biggest pieces of the individual journey in for both Katie and Nia was differentiating from one another. When we truly understand that we have space to explore, we can move from needing the approval of the systems or relationships we are a part of to understanding that what we need to give ourselves and how we need to show love to ourselves might not necessarily elicit approval from those same relationships and systems, and that is okay.

For many of us, enmeshment in relationships and the systems we're a part of seems like an easy option at first glance. We can evade identity-building by defaulting to our partner's preferences and identity. We can avoid rocking the boat in our relationships with friends by deferring to the other, forming a singular identity while never really understanding our individual selves. We may even accept rules and regulations that are present inside the systems we inhabit, even when everything within us screams that this is not who we are. It may be to avoid judgment, or we may truly be seeking the approval of our loved ones or our systems at large. This enmeshment in relationships and inside our systems may all feel like necessary steps to living our lives.

NIA LEAN-IN: As someone who lived most of my life in hiding, scared to look too closely at myself for fear of what I might find and what it might cost me, I resorted to studying others. I grew up fascinated by people, wondering what made them do what they did, trying to understand how relationships work, and digging into personality differences. Looking back, it's obvious that I was searching for myself in all of this work, and ultimately it was because of this work that I believe I was able to uncover my true identity. One of the big pieces to this puzzle was learning about the Enneagram of Personality.

For me, understanding myself through this personality typing system was key. The Enneagram of Personality system differs from other personality typing systems in that most systems focus on the behavior of a person, while the Enneagram focuses on the motivation behind the behavior. For me, this meant looking, nonjudgmentally, at why I do what I do. In particular, as an Enneagram 9, the peacemaker, why did I always default to my spouse's and friends' preferences and identities? A small example of this is, if I was asked where I wanted to go to lunch, without fail, I would say, "I don't care." Most of the time, this wasn't because I actually didn't care where we went to lunch; it was because I couldn't own my own story. And I couldn't own my own story because I didn't know it.

Digging into my own motivation, the *why* behind my preference to defer to other people's stories, ultimately was the first step on my own journey in. I didn't know who I was at all, so it was easy for me to defer. This lack of self-differentiation, not just in small things, would leave me with canned responses when people would ask me who I was. And I would almost always respond with a label that would tell my story in relation to someone else. I am a parent to my kids. I am a spouse to my wife. I am an employee of my employer. And while yes, I was all of those things, I never started with who I was on my own because my identity was buried so deep, and I truly didn't know.

As I made the journey in, I slowly started to find myself. I am someone who loves deep conversation with people. I am someone who enjoys lying in the grass on a sunny day. I am someone who loves color. It was through these little things, these small understandings of who I am, that I was eventually able to work toward the bigger, core identity pieces of myself. I am Queer. I am a transgender woman. Understanding my motivation was key to owning my story. I had to know it to own it. Now, if you ever go out to lunch with me and you ask me what I want, I will tell you what I am in the mood for, confident in the small things as well as the big things.

But eventually, deferring to others, defaulting to the way things are, allowing systems to impose themselves on us, and not following that inner scream to get out become harder and harder. To truly move forward in our identity-building, we need to detach from judgment, detach from expectation of others, and listen to ourselves. It's only then that we can start to move out, away, in, forward, or whatever way we truly decide we want to go.

Finding Queer Joy

One aspect of the journey in that often gets overlooked is the joy that can be found along the way. Identity-building may produce some of the most challenging moments of our lives, but inside of those moments, our seedling identity may sprout unexpectedly. Within the context of Queer identity and within Queer circles, much has been written about Queer joy. *Queer Insider*, an independent LGBTQ+ publication, describes Queer joy as "the deep happiness that brings warmth and purpose to [Q]ueer lives."[5]

Oftentimes, the building of Queer identity feels like a fight against ourselves and against the world, but finding those moments of Queer joy allows us to continue to move forward without getting overwhelmed. Finding Queer joy during our identity-building process is easier than it seems, but we have to stop and look for it as it may present itself in unexpected places.

For Nia, looking into the mirror for the first time and seeing herself clearly was one of those moments. Up until then, the mirror held negative connotations and the expectations of others, but when she looked up and could see herself clearly as the woman she is, there was joy. It felt like a fleeting moment in the midst of all the upheaval in her life, but it was something that she could return to. Even when we don't find Queer joy in the natural course of our typical days, we may be able to find it by seeking it out. Going to a drag brunch with friends or watching *Heartstopper* on Netflix[6] can bring us a dose of Queer joy when we need it.

Queer joy lives inside of us too. As someone discovering our Queer identity, we start to realize our joy is Queer joy. Sometimes it comes out in the form of dancing, singing, or laughing with friends and family. Ultimately, it is about being present in our journey in. When we start to uncover who we are, we can sit and be present with our expanding self. Many times, we first must be present to the pain and shame that surround us, but then slowly, we can start to notice things that bring us joy. The journey in takes practicing that presence. If we persist in that practice, then we, too, can join Prairie Johnson, the fictional character from the TV series *The OA*, in declaring, "I didn't disappear. I was present for all of it."[7]

Understanding Where We Want to Go from Here

Now that we've started the journey in; found a trusted, licensed therapist; have people and systems around us that will encourage our continued growth; have started to listen to ourselves; self-differentiate and practice presence in our lives, where do we go from here?

First, we must say that each Queer identity journey is different. This may seem obvious, but we can never overlay our journey directly on top of someone else's, even though they may seem like they are almost identical. When Nia was trying to decide what was next, determining whether or not to come out to Katie and others, she was able to find comfort and guidance in the stories of people who had gone before. Those stories, though, were made up of other people's experiences.

Understanding herself through those stories only took her so far. At some point, she had to own her own story in order to move forward.

Going forward does require self-trust. There will be moments when the shame is so overwhelming that it seems impossible to move forward, but we now know too much about ourselves to go back. These are the moments when we have to trust who we are and, with the help of our therapist and support system, make decisions about our journey, forgiving ourselves when necessary. Once we can rely on our own judgment again, or maybe for the first time, we can move forward, continuing to build our identity. As we journey in and our identity starts to unfurl and take shape, we have to let in some of our people on our newfound self. Going back to ring theory and our support network, we can find those people who are in the family and community circles who not only are encouraging of our growth but are also Queer-affirming people who will be there for us as we move forward. Deliberately letting those people in on who we are, even if we're still figuring that out, is the next big step on our journey.

Exercise

Projection Exercise for Decision-Making

Write a narrative that describes what life would be like if it were the same as it is now for the rest of your life.

Write a narrative that describes what life would be like if you were to make a decision—coming out to friends and family, for example—and live the rest of your life inside of that decision.

4

Letting Loved Ones In

NIA LEAN-IN: We were standing in the kitchen discussing the popular TV show *RuPaul's Drag Race*. The moment is frozen in my mind. Sami, Katie's sister and my sister-in-law, was extolling the virtues of the show while at the same time letting me know that she thought one of our sons, the performer, would do well on it. While being a drag queen didn't necessarily correlate to my own newly discovered identity as a Queer person—I hadn't yet realized I was transgender—I saw an opening to let her in on who I was. I remember, before I spoke, understanding I had a brief opportunity to share who I was before the moment passed. How, though, could I turn this conversation about drag queens into revealing my Queer identity for the first time? I drew a breath and responded, "Well, why do you think he'd be the best drag queen in the house? I think I would be pretty good at it." Not fully understanding what was happening but knowing this was a moment of authenticity between us, she pressed in.

"Would you ever do it?"

"Yeah, I would," I replied.

In those three words, I revealed myself to Sami that day in our kitchen. Neither of us knew what it meant fully, but I knew in that moment before I spoke that she was a safe person. I could reveal a part of myself to her, even a part of my identity that I was still building. I could tell her what I knew to be true about myself, which at that point was only that I was different.

She responded simply, "Cool." I don't remember what else we talked about, but I do remember a huge weight being lifted off my shoulders. I had let someone close to me in on my journey. Nothing and everything changed that day. Even though I had no idea how this moment would launch me down a road to much broader self-discovery, I did feel free. Someone else besides my spouse knew me as much as I knew me, and she was willing to walk with me as I discovered more of myself.

Letting In

We've reached the *letting in* portion of our Queer identity-building journey. Letting in differs from coming out to others because most of the time when we let others in on who we are at a particular moment, we are still in the process of major self-discovery. Coming out tends to present a more formed identity to the world, while letting in is a process in which we can gather safe and supportive people around us, let them in on what we currently know about ourselves, and let them support us as we continue to search for who we are. It is a time of fluidity and uncertainty when we decide to trust others with ourselves.

LETTING LOVED ONES IN

To let others in, we must first return to our circles of support. Remember, we've already identified people in our family and community who should be ready and willing to love us fiercely without guilt or shame, but now we invite people in further. We create a firm inner circle of people, some who may have been on the outside of our support circles previously and others who are already closest to us, by letting those select few people in on who we are becoming.

This process, although tricky and often fraught with worry and doubt, is one of the most intuitive in our identity-building. Trusting our instincts about who is safe and who is not, and who will support our identity-building and who will not, should be a priority.

When to Let Others In

The first question that may arise about the letting-in process might be "How do I know when to let other people in?" This is a question Nia asked her therapist during some of her initial sessions. She wondered how she would know when it was time to get more support for herself during this journey through the friends and family in her inner circles. Her therapist responded with an apt metaphor. Just like a teakettle needs to release steam when the water is boiling, in the same way, Nia would instinctively know when it was time to let others in on her identity. This answer at first seemed like not an answer at all, and for Nia, who was in therapy seeking answers, it didn't seem very helpful. But her therapist's insistence that "you'll know when you know," in the end, proved to be exactly right.

No one knows but ourselves when it's time to open up to others. Only we can feel the mounting pressure inside us. The need to be seen and supported by others rises up so strongly in us that it spurs us to action. This is when we must trust ourselves and act.

NIA LEAN-IN: I remember my first teakettle moment like it was yesterday. I didn't yet fully know what my Queer identity was or what it meant for my life, but I knew I had to do something with whatever was bubbling up inside of me. I had to let Katie, my spouse, in on what was happening. On my thirty-fourth birthday, the pressure inside of me had built to the point where the steam had nowhere to go but out. The teakettle whistled loud and long. In fact, I just looked back at that day on our electronic family calendar, and one of us had written "hope when you need it most" right next to a reminder that we'd be going on a date for my birthday. I'm not sure why we wrote that on the calendar, but little did I know how true that was.

That night, Katie gave me a gift. Having been together for fourteen years at that point, we knew each other well. She knew that I am a creature of comfort. I love sitting in the warm sun in a field of green, and I would lie in a hammock with a good book for my job if I could. She also knows my comfort extends to the things I wear. So with that in mind, she gave me a thoughtful gift. I opened it that night, completely unsure of what it was, although she had been talking it up all day. To my surprise, it was undershirts and pajama pants—not regular undershirts and pajama pants, mind you, but the comfortable, soft, kind. The kind that most guys would say about in a deep, gruff voice, "Uh, what are you trying to say about me?" I think the word *luxurious* was actually printed on the packaging of both items. My beautiful, thoughtful wife just wanted me to know she saw me. But what did my steamy, teakettle self do with this thoughtful gift? I complained. I immediately launched into a diatribe about how, while it was a thoughtful gift, it wasn't enough. I wanted more. More softness, more femininity. A strange turn of conversation for her, I'm sure. I was basically telling her I wished she had really seen what was going on with me, even though I didn't know, and that I wished she had gotten me a skirt and halter top so I could be a real woman, not this pretend version of femininity that she was handing me. Thanks for nothing! I couldn't understand what was going on with myself, so I projected it on to her.

I'm asked all the time when I tell people I am a transgender person, "Did you know your whole life? Has this been with you always? Or did you just figure this out?" This is the single most common question I have gotten so far.

My trans identity has, in fact, been with me my whole life, but to say I "knew" what was going on would be disingenuous. Several people whom I have told about myself have said to me, "Oh, I think that makes sense based on some of my interactions with you." And while they can never quite say which interactions they're talking about that showed them I was a woman living life as a man, this is almost exactly how I feel about my own life.

Looking back, there were points in my life that I see in hindsight as signposts for what was to come, but in the moment, there was no way for me to put any of it together. It felt like a left-handed child being told to write with their right hand because that's what everyone is supposed to do. I learned to act and behave like a man, quite well in fact, but something felt off. For me, something didn't quite feel complete.

That night, thirty-four years of repression and living up to other people's expectations came spilling out in one fell swoop on my wife. I knew, or thought I knew, our love could handle it. I instinctively knew she would help me understand what I didn't even know I was telling her. Also, she was the one person in my life who I knew was safe to let in at that moment, no matter where we ended up. And the safety she provided led me to be a real jerk that night. Little did we both know that the safety she provided for me that night would also give me the space to go on my identity-building journey. I'm so grateful for the way she saw me that night and how she responded to me letting her in on my journey. I'm grateful for the way she has seen me our entire lives because that seeing has allowed me to be who I am.

Whom to Let In

When determining whom to let in on our personal journey, we should first think about safety. Who will give us the most physical and psychological safety, along with the support we need to continue the hard work of identity-building? While close friends and family may be safe, it may be more helpful to first reveal our journey to someone nearer the outer part of the circle of support or even someone who might be outside of our current orbit. People inside our inner circles are more likely to have strong emotional reactions to our news, whether positive or negative, simply because they are more invested in our lives. By choosing someone who is more detached from our life, someone who is not enmeshed with our own identity, it will be easier for us to draw a boundary if things do not go as planned.

The very first person Nia let in on her journey, aside from Katie, was a former coworker, Kassie. Nia understood this former coworker to be a safe and welcoming person, and in the case that things had changed, there was not a big risk to Nia's psychological or physical safety because she wasn't in a day-to-day relationship with Kassie. Kassie was a trusted friend from a past company, someone at arm's length from Nia's everyday life but still a friend whom Nia hoped would understand this revelation about her identity and could support her in her journey. As it turned out, Kassie was a great choice as the first person for Nia to let in.

Another consideration when choosing whom to let in on our journey is that person's own circle of support. Does the person we are letting in have their own support network outside of ours that they can utilize if they have a strong emotional reaction to our revelation? And can they be trusted to use their own network of support when needed? How much do our support networks overlap? By choosing someone who has their own circle of support, our support person will be better positioned to help us. They are someone who is more differentiated from our own story.

After Nia made her initial lists of who should be in her circle of support, she made three more lists of who needed to be let in on her journey while it was still developing. The first list was a group of people who were the furthest removed from Nia's everyday life. They would be safe and have their own support network to process any difficulty they had with the news. They were people to whom Nia could reveal her identity as a work in progress and who would be able to give her the space to continue growing. Their own support systems were almost completely outside of Nia's, although at times, they might overlap a little. Thinking about each of our own circles of support as planetary systems, the first group of people were on the outside of Nia's everyday orbit and included people like Kassie (Figure 3).

The second list of people were also trustworthy—more on assuming people's trust and reactions later—but many in this group were closer friends and family. Their reaction to the news might be stronger, but they also had their own support, different from Nia's, even though their circles may have overlapped more than the first group. For Nia, Sami was the first in this group, someone whose life overlapped with Nia's in many more ways than Kassie's had but who was self-differentiated, trustworthy, and could process any emotional reactions with someone outside of Nia's orbit (Figure 4).

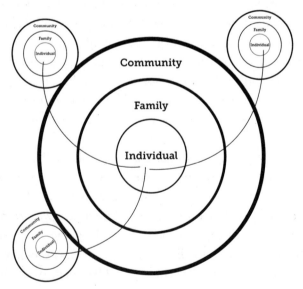

Figure 3: Outside Support

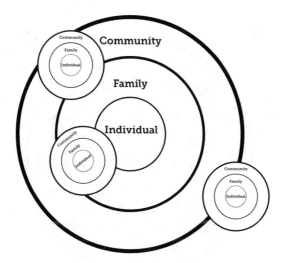

Figure 4: Inside Support

These first two lists would become the framework for stable circles of support. Identifying people in all layers of the circle of support who could be pulled into the letting-in process early allowed Nia to have a strong level of safety, security, and support throughout the rest of the coming-out process.

Another way to visualize or identify those people whom we can let in on our journey is to depict them as stars within our circles of support. The first list identifies those stars outside of our circles, and the second list identifies stars closer to the middle of our circles (Figure 5).

During the letting-in process, we can pull those stars in close in order to shelter and support us while we build our identity. This group will be the ones who hold us up even when things get difficult or confusing and are there to help us process and discover ourselves in the early stages. This grouping of star supporters becomes our *circle of safety* (Figure 6). Beyond our normal

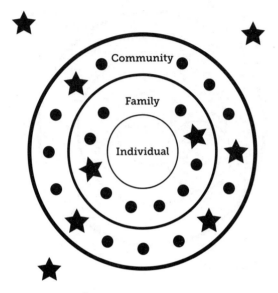

Figure 5: Stars in Our Circles

circles of support, this circle of safety becomes a refuge and helps us and can assist us in becoming more ourselves because they provide the safety necessary to explore ourselves more deeply.

The third list that Nia made was people who needed to be let in on her identity while it was still forming due to their proximity in her life. These were people who weren't necessarily safe. Fortunately, there were not many on this list for Nia, but for some of us, this list may be longer. If we're experimenting with gender expression in our own home, we may have to let our spouse, partner, or housemate in on our journey even if they may not be supportive. We may want to be the ones to tell our family of origin about our unfolding Queer identity before it is fully formed simply to make sure that we are the ones to talk to them before they hear the news from someone else. If this group

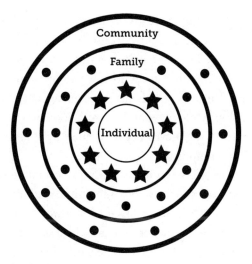

Figure 6: Circle of Safety

of people proves to be unsafe during the letting-in process, we'll have to draw firm boundaries.

How to Let Others In

Once Nia had her list, the question became how to let others in. What did this look like? What can we say? Should we take a friend out for coffee and blurt out our innermost thoughts, or should we write a letter or email and send it off without explanation? There seemed to be so many options for communicating something that felt so important. Again, this is where we must return to trusting our own instincts. We are all different people, different communicators, and we have different needs and desires for our own personal journeys. We must learn to trust ourselves here.

Many of us who are ready to let others in on our changing and growing Queer identity begin by looking for openings. We look for space in everyday interactions where we can let our friend or family member know who we are without forcing the conversation. This can be exhausting, causing us to miss out on real relationship while we look to position ourselves, and many times these openings never occur. It may help if we are more thoughtful in our approach.

There is no right or wrong way to let others in; however, there are ways that can maximize our safety and support and allow us to draw boundaries in the face of a strong emotional reaction. Nia started her letting-in process with Kassie through Facebook Messenger. It had been a while since they had talked, and Nia reconnected first. She then let Kassie know that she had a changing Queer identity and asked for a specific form of support: help with makeup lessons. The specificity in this request allowed Kassie to accept or reject Nia's request without much emotion. Kassie accepted Nia's request and was so welcoming and excited to learn more about Nia's journey, just what Nia had hoped for.

KASSIE LEAN-IN: When Nia first asked me for makeup advice, I didn't think twice about it. I was excited she had reached out to me for advice. I actually thought she just wanted to perform in a drag show and was happy to help. The day I met Nia, we just clicked, and she's been a friend ever since. It truly meant the world that she confided in me when the time was right for her. I can't imagine how hard it may have been for her going through everything. I'm so glad that I am a part of her journey and have been able to watch her stay true to herself and move toward happiness.

With Sami, Nia found an inroad through natural conversation. When the moment presented itself during their discussion about *RuPaul's Drag Race*, Nia seized the opportunity to let Sami in. This was less calculated than the conversation with Kassie but served the same purpose. It was a moment for Nia to be her authentic self, allowing Sami to see all of her, and in fact served to grow their relationship. Sami would comment afterward that she felt as though she never really knew Nia until that moment in their relationship.

SAMI LEAN-IN: When Nia let me in on who she was, I saw her for the first time. I hadn't explored our relationship up to this point because I think my own childhood trauma allows me to pick up on secret-keepers and feel cautious about asking for more information. I could sense Nia holding on to something before she let me in. It also might be because we never before had a relationship where we shared anything with each other. Because of this lack of relationship, I feel like when she told me about who she was, I was let in on seeing her as a whole rather than just my sister's partner and that she saw me not just as a sister-in-law but as a friend to be trusted.

There are countless other ways to let people in on our blossoming Queer identities, but again we must return to our instincts. With a little planning and a lot of trust in ourselves, we will be able to build a support system of stars who can continue to help us grow into who we are rather than starting with people who resist our continued growth and who may harm us in the process.

Allowing Space

Letting people in on who we are, no matter what part of ourselves we are revealing, Queer or otherwise, takes courage. In those moments of courage, we draw a breath, tell our story, and then wait. The moments in between revealing ourselves to someone and their response can seem like an eternity. We've put ourselves out there. We've been vulnerable with a friend, colleague, or family member, and now they will react to that vulnerability. As much as we might try to create the right conditions and find the right people to be vulnerable with, there is no controlling how people will react. We may even think we know exactly how our vulnerability will land with someone, but truly we don't know.

Nia learned an important lesson very early on during her letting-in process, and that was that she could not prejudge other people's reactions to the news about her Queer identity. There were a few people out of the gate whom she let in on her journey simply because they were in close proximity to her in daily life, but she wasn't sure if they were safe. One person she thought would not be as safe turned out to be supportive and affirming. Another person whom she thought would be immediately safe and supportive did not react that way initially and ended up taking some time and conversation before they expressed the level of support and care that she had hoped for.

Prejudging people tends to build up conversations and let us down when things don't go as planned. We never can truly know how our story is going to bump up against the story of the person we're speaking with, in positive and negative ways. There may be something within our story that is triggering for our friend, or it may be the first time they've known a Queer individual. People have the reactions that they have to our letting-in process for all sorts of reasons, and us projecting their response doesn't change what will actually happen.

Learning this early on in Nia's process allowed her to simply own her story and let others' responses be what they were as she moved forward. This proved to be very beneficial and allowed her to reject people's negative narrative of her, which happened more often during the coming-out process. For those who are hearing from a Queer person, we will include some of the kindest responses and emails that Nia received from people during the letting-in and coming-out processes in the toolkit at the back of the book. There are many ways to show someone you care, but these particular responses to Nia's Queer identity stand out as thoughtful, meaningful, and supportive in ways Nia couldn't have imagined.

When we share who we are with a loved one, in the moments between our vulnerability and their response, it may seem that our very personhood hangs in the balance. Take a deep breath. Feel the liberation inherent in this moment. No matter the reaction, we have accomplished something. We have made ourselves known, and it can be one of the most freeing experiences in the world. Linger in the moment and don't prepare for what comes next because we don't know what that is, and we can't control it.

When we finally do get a response, it may or may not be what we had hoped for. Either way, we must allow space for the person we are letting in to feel and own their own feelings, just as we are feeling and owning ours. This means allowing for an affirming, disbelieving, or doubtful response. No matter what, the response does not belong to us, even though it may feel like it is an indictment of who we are. Allowing those whom we are letting in to have their own emotions and their own response is critical for being able to move forward.

Creating Strong Boundaries

We hope that when we're vulnerable with someone and let them in on our journey, they immediately affirm who we are, create a safe space for us to continue our journey, and process their own emotions with people outside of our mutual circles. For those people who have such an affirming response, we can express our appreciation and continue to grow in relationship with them, moving forward together. However, this is not always the case. Again, we can't know how people will react, so we must be prepared to create strong boundaries when necessary. And while we may be unfamiliar with drawing boundaries, when things don't go as planned, we must return to self-differentiation. We must own our own story first, self-differentiate, and explicitly express our needs.

Self-differentiation during the letting-in process starts with viewing our loved one's feelings as separate from our own. We don't own their feelings, and we aren't responsible for them. When a loved one responds with a question like "What does this mean for me?" we must understand that we can't answer that question. We might know what it means for us in that moment, and we can communicate that if we do, but we can't answer their questions about how this news affects their identity. We can simply return to who we are, who we have just told them we are, and encourage them to find the support they need to process their own emotions.

Expressing our own needs in the moment may be helpful. Explicitly requesting that our loved ones own their own feelings, as well as process those feelings with others outside of our orbit, may feel harsh at first, but it ultimately makes our needs clear. As Brené Brown says, clear is kind.[1] We may need to have a conversation regarding whom we would and would not like our loved one to process our news with. For the conversation with Sami, for instance, it would have been helpful for Nia to express, "Please process this with your friends but not your dad." Sami knew this instinctively, and Nia trusted Sami, but being explicit about desires and needs during the letting-in process is always best.

Beyond owning our story, self-differentiating, and explicitly expressing our needs, there may be moments when we need to draw hard lines in the sand. Hopefully, we are letting in people who are safe, those stars who will make space and push our circles of support out wider for our continued self-discovery, but again, there may be times when we need to let people in on who we are simply due to the nature of the relationship or their proximity to our lives.

When those people prove to be unsafe, we must be clear. Words and actions that harm are unacceptable to us, and if we can't have a conversation without harmful words or actions, we need to stop having conversations. We can again encourage our loved ones to get the support they need, but continuing to engage in a harmful relationship can not only hinder our ability to grow but it can also do significant harm to our mental and emotional states. There may be even moments when physical harm is a possibility. In these cases, it may be helpful to have another trusted person with us when we let someone in on who we are.

Mental, emotional, physical, and spiritual abuses are never acceptable forms of reactionary responses to our vulnerability. When they happen, we need to be prepared to halt relationships in the moment and possibly return to them when cooler heads prevail. For some relationships, healing and reconciliation will happen over time. For others, the damage may go much deeper and require separation for an indefinite period of time. Again, owning our story is key here. Knowing who we are and protecting ourselves, our own inner child—just like we would a child who is external to us—help us to create our own environment of safety and security.

Our loved ones may require space in this process, and that's okay. Ideally, they can find that space through other relationships, therapists, or organizations that support the loved ones of Queer individuals. Stepping away from a relationship for a time or creating distance to give the other person space to process is a natural step for many. The time and distance can allow for ruptures to heal and relationships to regain their footing.

For others who want to process our news with us or ask us questions that aren't ours to answer—like "How could you do this to me?"—we can simply say no. We can't be the person to process with them. We can't be the one to answer questions that they should own instead of us. We don't need to be apologetic; we just need to own our story. This may mean taking a step away and allowing things to heal in order to move forward together, but it may also mean distance in a relationship that never resolves or even the end to a relationship that once seemed strong.

Journeying Together

When we let others in on who we are and they affirm the identity work we've done, are able to own their own story, and get the support they need in order to continue down the road of relationship with us, we can work toward individual growth on our journey together. Journeying together means that we have to be okay and accepting when someone says something they don't mean but is willing to come back and say *I'm sorry*. It means being able to accept that our awareness of our identities change and that we are now a part of that for each other.

Nia felt bad when she came back to Sami months later and said that in fact she was not interested in drag, but she is transgender. It felt to her like she had lied during the initial letting in. But being true to our identity doesn't always mean understanding the whole picture all at once. It's not until further down the road that we may gain the clarity to understand our previous identity stage to its fullest extent. This process means being gentle with ourselves and each other, as well as forgiving missteps and honoring growth.

Supporting each other also means being a soft place to land. For those of us who are letting others in on our journey, there will be hard times. Having someone, those stars, there to comfort, encourage, and just sit with us can be a cornerstone to helping us discover who we are. Love can look like a lot of different things, but finding those people whom we trust with ourselves, even when we don't know ourselves fully, will be key to continuing on our journey.

Reflection

Make a list of people who can be let in on your journey and reflect:

* ✳ Do these people have their own circles of support?
* ✳ Can these people be trusted with my identity as a work in progress?

✴   What support can these people give me on my journey?

Sort the people above into three lists:

List 1	List 2	List 3
People who are stars outside of my current orbit who are safe to let in on my journey	People who are stars inside of my current orbit who are safe to let in on my journey	People who are inside of my current orbit who may not be stars but who should be let in on my journey due to proximity

5

The Individual
Journey Out

NIA LEAN-IN: The moment came one October, a nearly perfect
day. It was a warm afternoon for fall in Iowa, sixty-eight degrees,
and the air was crisp. If it hadn't been a Monday, it would have
been perfect. I took a break from work and looked down at my
phone to find some social media notifications. As I clicked to
see what was going on, I realized that the current US president
had done something to roll back protections for transgender
individuals. The headlines read something like this one from
the *New York Times*: "'Transgender' Could Be Defined Out of
Existence under the Trump Administration." The article went
on to describe how "the Trump administration [was] considering
narrowly defining gender . . . the most drastic move yet in a
governmentwide effort to roll back recognition and protections of
transgender people under federal civil rights law."[1] In essence, the
president wanted to change the stance of the federal government
so that gender was defined as an immutable, biological condition

determined by genitalia at birth, which would eliminate gender protections for millions of transgender people.

I paused for a moment to consider this. I had already let Katie and a few other select people in on my journey, but I wasn't out as a transgender woman and wasn't planning to come out anytime soon. I wasn't practically affected by any move to restrict civil rights of trans people. I got online to post about it from my perceived perspective as a straight, white male, to be angry for my transgender friends, but I couldn't do it. This was connected to my very being in ways that I couldn't speak to by simply being angry for my friends. The frustration that I couldn't say anything to my family and friends about this from the perspective of a transgender woman, because no one knew I was a transgender woman, rose rapidly inside me. A thought quickly flashed through my mind. *What if I told them I was transgender?* I hoped that if I was able to speak up about an issue from a more personal perspective, I could change the hearts and minds of my family and friends on the issue.

This brief thought and feeling of hope provided the courage for me to send an email to my siblings, parents, and in-laws telling them who I am. With courage and blind adrenaline, I quickly sent the emails, closed my computer, and left work, unsure of what I had just done and unaware of how it would change the course of my life. That night, as I waited for something, anything, by way of response from all of them, I knew something had changed. The biggest pressure valve to date had been released. A huge weight had been lifted. And although it was replaced by a smaller weight of relationships in the balance, I knew there was no going back. The steam was out of the kettle, and I felt so relieved.

A Queer Timeline

While our metaphorical teakettle may have been bubbling during our journey inward and whistling off and on during the letting-in process, by the time we've reached the journey out and the coming-out process, it is whistling like international grand champion whistler Sean Lomax—yes, this is a real thing, and you should definitely Google it.

For many Queer individuals, coming out is the defining moment during the journey out. It is the time in our lives when, after journeying in and letting a select few in on our growth and change, we decide to openly share our Queer identity with the world. But the coming-out process isn't linear. In fact, even the concept of a timeline itself—the straight line with seminal moments plotted with dots—becomes Queered during this process. While our life seemingly continues to move forward in time, our journey takes all sorts of twists and turns. It's more like a jumbled mess of squiggles.

In truth, all of our lives include these twists and turns, but the Queer journey only magnifies this. We've been inside ourselves, learning who we are for some time on the journey in. As we start to make our way out, we let others in who can support us, and our awareness of our identity changes and shifts. Over time, that group of stars in our inner circle grows large, and our identity feels more solidly formed. We feel as though we can tell the world who we are, and we come out, pronouncing our identity to the world. But then our awareness of our identity may shift again, and we feel like we're back at square one. Even if we feel like we have a solid foothold on who we are and are settled having come out to the world at large, many of us have to come out over and over again, every time we meet new people. It can be exhausting. This process also looks different for everyone, depending on circumstances, background, experience, and our own journey in and letting-in processes. No matter who you are, though, take your time and trust yourself because while the journey in fortifies our mettle, the journey out tests its strength in every way.

Self-Acceptance

While the *journey out* follows different paths for all of us, the defining moment that shifts us from an inward stance to one that is moving outward is self-acceptance. This may happen suddenly, at any time, and in unexpected ways. For Nia, there were multiple moments, especially during therapy, when cutting through the shame of internalized Queerphobia produced self-acceptance, but none more pronounced than the day she came out to her family. Something switched inside of her that day from "I think this is who I am" to "I know this is who I am, and I am good."

Individuals who aren't Queer may also recognize this feeling of self-acceptance. Perhaps we discover our true identity while attending an AA meeting, processing the trauma of childhood with a therapist, or revealing a hidden part of ourselves to a close friend. It is a moment of clarity when we know who we are, and no one can tell us differently. We know we are someone to be celebrated, and we can walk forward in life with that confidence. Some of us experience self-acceptance in a single dramatic moment, but for many of us, self-acceptance arises thanks to a series of little moments until one day we open our eyes to the person we've become and realize it is who we were made to be. For Nia, again, it was both. Many small moments led to the moment when the switch flipped, and she came out to her family.

Moving forward on the journey out requires strength. We may be at a point of self-acceptance, but depending on what we've been through in our lives, it may take time to gather the strength to be able to move. We spoke with musical artist Semler recently and asked them what they would say to their younger self in regard to the journey in, letting in, and the journey out. They said they would remind their younger self to face the things that scare them but to "take the time to feel strong enough to do it."[2] Jumping into coming out when we're not ready but because we think we need to mirror the journey of someone else can be harmful if we're not strong enough to hold our boundaries to protect ourselves and cope with the change that is coming.

Who, What, When, Where, and Why

Once we have gathered enough self-acceptance and strength inside of our bodies, we may be at a point where we feel the need and desire to come out to the world at large. Getting to a point where we are comfortable and capable of coming out, self-disclosing our sexual and/or gender identity to the world, is no small feat. We've worked hard to build our identity and our circles of support around us, and now we want to show the world who we are. For some, this moment never happens. It may be impossible due to life circumstances that prevent disclosure. There are a number of reasons Queer people don't come out, from the possibility of job loss to family abandonment to physical harm. For those who have been pulled into circles of support for these Queer individuals as they build their identity, understand that you can support your loved one by just being with them. It can be extremely painful to be unable to express who we are fully to the world, and having a support system around us can be a lifeline to hold us up. Circumstances may or may not change over time for these individuals, but ultimately not being "out" about our Queer identity doesn't invalidate our identity in any way.

For those who do have the opportunity to reveal themselves to the world, the details of who, what, when, where, and how are very personal. It may look very similar to the letting-in process we've just gone through; however, coming out tends to present a more formed identity to the world. The tipping point of when our identity is formed enough is up to us. Much has been written about coming out, but two resources we recommend are The Trevor Project's *The Coming Out Handbook* and the book *Unashamed: A Coming-Out Guide for LGBTQ Christians* by Amber Cantorna. Tools like these can be useful throughout our journey in, the letting-in process, and for coming out—particularly as we set expectations for others.

Setting Expectations

Owning our story and returning to our boundaries are key for setting expectations during our coming-out process. Standing tall in our new Queer identity by owning our story can help people who are supportive know how we expect them to interact with us on our journey moving forward. And for people who are less supportive of our Queer identity, we can return to the skill of boundary-making, in which we may have gotten a lot of practice during the letting-in process.

We will have to set all kinds of expectations for others, but one of the most important is language. For people who are new to understanding the LGBTQIA+ rainbow, language can be one of the most daunting challenges. Many people are afraid they won't know what to say and will say the wrong thing, and many times this is true. Especially if we are the first Queer person our loved one has known, there will be a learning curve. We may need to clarify for people the difference between sex and gender. For those of us with new names and pronouns, we can clearly communicate these and create safe spaces for our loved ones to fail as they earnestly try to respect us by calling us by our names.

Sometimes, when we come out on a whim or when the opportunity presents itself, we don't have the opportunity to discuss expectations in advance. In these cases, it can be helpful to circle back to clarify our expectations and set the tone for how we should be treated going forward. This is about conveying our story and how we deserve to be treated but not about justifying our existence.

Many times, marginalized communities are asked to educate the masses in order for people to be more sensitive to our stories. This includes justifying our existence in the world. That is not what we are talking about here when we are setting the tone. There are other resources to help people better understand that Queer people have the right to exist and should be valued for who we are, and we do not have to be that resource in this moment. When explaining the difference between sex and gender to someone turns into defending our right to exist, we can take a step back and give our loved ones a myriad of online and other resources that can help educate them. We do not have to justify our existence in this moment.

But for our friends who are willing to lean into our stories and ask honest questions, hoping to gain a better understanding of who we are, setting the tone by sharing our stories and educating when we have the chance can be fun. Nia recently had a conversation with a good friend and mentor, Laura, about the word *Queer*. Laura, a cis, straight woman, was uncomfortable with the word *Queer* as she had come up in an era when the word was used in a deliberate way to harm the LGBTQIA+ community. Nia had the conversation with Laura about why she uses the word *Queer* for her own identity and let Laura know that it was okay for her to use it when referring to Nia and Nia's story. This kind of explicit communication can set the tone for positive interactions and relationship-building in the future and hopefully will lead us to feeling seen and heard in ways we have never felt before. Since that conversation, Laura has confirmed she is getting more comfortable with the word Queer, driven by the open conversation and Nia's willingness to share her experience.

For those of us who have more people in our lives who want to push back on our identity rather than listen to our stories, it can wear us down quickly. Being clear, setting boundaries, and walking away from conversation can become very tiring, very quickly. At times, it can seem like even people we don't know are pushing back against our being. Politicians are legislating against our bodies and our rights, the news media is debating our validity, and for those of us who are visibly, outwardly Queer, even people in the grocery store seem to be giving us sideways glances that feel like they are pushing back on our existence. This is where we have to rely on the support network we've built previously. We have those stars around us whom we can go to when the going—or the coming out, in this case— gets tough.

Coping with Change

Returning to our circles of safety and particularly our stars in times of stress and exhaustion can be a key form of self-care during the coming-out process. This is especially true for those of us who come out inside of larger systems where our identity is not just debated but flatly denied. Calling one of our stars to meet us at a coffee shop to process through our feelings or just to come over to watch Netflix is an easy way to regain our footing when it feels too rocky to stand up inside of our Queer identity.

These friends can not only be there for us with comfort and care but can also give us assistance in holding boundaries and standing up for ourselves when we need it. More than once during Nia's coming-out process, she grabbed one of her stars and asked them to join her as she had a hard conversation with someone else when she anticipated having to defend her identity. Friends and family who can support and give advice to us while we're in the middle of the crisis and deeply emotional states are a required support for the journey out.

Change of this magnitude will certainly be accompanied by all sorts of emotions, but *relief* is often the most prominent emotion we experience after revealing ourselves to the world. Many of us have spent our entire lives either consciously hiding away from the world or repressing our own Queer identities from ourselves. After a lifetime of keeping our true selves bottled up, we'll likely feel an immediate sense of relief from telling others who we are.

This feeling may last a long time but is certain to eventually be replaced by something else. Maybe anger as we watch the world around us be unkind to Queer people. Perhaps a sadness that we weren't able to express our Queer identity sooner.

For others, especially the genderqueer among us, the next thing we may feel is an intense feeling of self-consciousness. Those of us who put the T in LGBTQ+ can feel immediately conspicuous after coming out, even in the simplest of tasks like stopping at the gas station. The never-ending sets of eyes that fall on a genderqueer person throughout our regular, everyday life can be exhausting. For most of us, that exhaustion is a price gladly paid to be able to be our full selves; however, we have to learn how to adjust and take care of ourselves.

NIA LEAN-IN: Coming out as transgender created an immediate sense of relief for me. I didn't realize how much mental space and energy I was spending on hiding myself from people, and stepping into just being myself allowed me to focus my energies on other things. Soon after coming out, I realized some of my energy had to be refocused on moving through the world in a new, conspicuous way. I can remember the first few times I felt conspicuous out in public after coming out as transgender. The first time, Katie and I were in an art museum gift shop. A woman came up to us and told me how "brave" I was for being out in public and then proceeded to tell us through tears about someone in her life who was transgender, culminating the conversation in a hug. This was new and definitely not something that I expected to happen when I came out to the world. The second time it happened, a woman followed me around in Target for a while, ultimately asking for my help finding a food item. I thought that was the end of the interaction, but in the checkout line, she approached me to invite me to a women's brunch she was having that weekend. For many, this may seem like such a small action, but to a budding trans woman, it not only affirmed my identity but also reinforced how conspicuous I was in my everyday life. After a few of these encounters, I realized that being conspicuous was something that I couldn't avoid and made a personal decision to lean into these encounters with people when they were positive and where I had the capacity to do so. You can read more about my conspicuous encounters with strangers on Medium.com, and although they have slowed down over the years, being conspicuous is now something that is a part of my everyday life.

Self-care becomes key to surviving after coming out as Queer, no matter who you are. Even for those who aren't conspicuous in our everyday lives, the emotional toll that coming out takes on us requires us to care for ourselves in ways we maybe haven't had to before. This, of course, looks different for everyone, but creating a proactive self-care routine after coming out is a must. Nia's favorite self-care during her initial coming out was going to a salt lounge with her good friend Kristin. It was a space where they could sit and decompress, with no pressures from the world around them, and where Nia felt she could just be.

These types of self-care moments proved to be even more necessary for Nia because one of the strongest emotions she experienced during the coming-out process was grief. Grief from not being accepted by all of her loved ones. Grief from not being able to be who she was for the first thirty-five years of her life. And maybe more surprisingly to her, grief over her changing identity.

NIA LEAN-IN: As a trans person whose awareness of myself changed drastically during my identity-building journey, I didn't expect to feel grief as deeply as I did throughout the process. I experienced the peak of my grief on a business road trip, driving alone in my car. It had been weeks and months since coming out as trans, and things were changing. The way I moved through the world was changing, my body was changing, and my relationships were changing. As I tried to process it all on my drive, the grief hit me all at once. I grieved broken relationships. I grieved my role in the world as it used to be, which was easy. I grieved the things I used to be able to do with my body that I now couldn't. And though I was so happy about who I was and who I was becoming, it didn't stop the grief. Processing through my grief in the long car ride that day ultimately led me to frustration and anger. I screamed at the top of my lungs. It was just once, but the emotion of it all created in me such a guttural scream that I lost my voice for most of the three days that I was on my business trip. Looking back, I now realize that acknowledging the grief and working through the frustration were so important for me to continue moving forward.

Perhaps one of the most surprising things for us as we journey through our identity process is that growth in our identity can bring about grief surrounding who we used to be. This is a normal process that comes with change but can still be jarring, frustrating, and tiring, to say the least. The process of accepting who we are now cannot fully reach its completion until we have shown ourselves to the world. When the metamorphosis is complete,[3] we can truly see how much we've changed, and some of that change might feel like loss. We will speak more about this type of loss in chapter 6.

Our new identity is fragile at this moment. Our insides, raw from all the work we've done, are now displayed vulnerably on the outside for the world to see and judge. This is why it's so important to do the hard work of journeying in and letting others in to support us as we grow. When we get to this moment in our journey, this scaffolding will hold us up and move us toward self-acceptance and the joy that we already started building on our journey in, as well as pride in our Queer identity.

Discovering Queer Community

If we're going to cope well with change, our community must grow. We must expand our trusted circles, growing from just a few stars whom we've pulled into our inner circle to finding new community. Up to this point on our journey, we've been asking friends and family for their support as we understand ourselves and grow, and now we can move into a broader community of mutual support. For many of us, the process of building our Queer identity may cost us friends, family, and even large parts of the communities we had been a part of. It's so important that we look to rebuild our community when this happens, and even for those who haven't lost any community, it's important to find community that can reflect us back to ourselves.

After Nia came out, a Queer community in our midwestern city of Des Moines was waiting with open arms. While moving into that community was scary and many times required a proactive approach to meeting people and making friends, it is one of the most rewarding communities to be a part of.

Not all Queer communities are created equal, and just like any community, Queer communities have issues with in-groups and out-groups, but when groups of Queer people get together, there is often joy. We've done the hard work to understand ourselves and have overcome hurdles and challenges to simply be ourselves, and the joy that can emanate from being free to be ourselves is palpable.

Queer Pride

Now that we're in community with other Queer people, we get the opportunity to sit back and realize how far we've come. We can also move from joy to pride. Queer pride is something that a person can never fully understand before going through this Queer identity-building process. But as we move into community and see ourselves reflected in others around us, we will see that we are not alone. The work we have done to get where we are was no small feat. Not only that, but getting to a place where we are more comfortable with who we are allows us to reflect on who we've been. It's this reflection that often causes us to well up with pride. We've had our moments of grief and can look back at who we used to be and compare that person with the person we are today. Pride in the work that we've accomplished and who we've become is a natural outflow of that reflection.

For many, the road to pride in our Queer identities is the culmination of a long journey. For so long, we've been unable to be who we are, hidden away from the world and oftentimes from ourselves. But now, we are free to simply be. And the simple act of being when we couldn't before brings us to a place of joy, satisfaction, and deep pride in who we are.

Celebration

Celebration is one of the hallmarks of Queer pride. Those who have attended a Pride parade understand this. The over-the-top nature of Pride celebration isn't because Queer people love fabulousness, although many times we do, but because we feel an innate and deep need to mark moments in time on our journey. This can occur annually during Pride month, which commemorates the Stonewall riots of 1969, an important moment in the history of the larger Queer community, or it can occur on a smaller individual scale.

As we move through our journey, it is important to take the time to stop and celebrate. Even before coming out, we should take time to pause and reflect on important moments in our journey, locking the significance of them in our minds. Nia's journey has included many important moments, but one in particular was a name-changing ceremony. For those who choose to change their name as part of their journey, it is a significant step in becoming confident in who we are and is one of those moments that can be acknowledged as a building block for our future. Gathering community around us during these moments is key, and experiencing these landmarks with loved ones allows us to hold on to a piece of our journey in a palpable way going forward.

The Work Ahead

Getting to a place where we're comfortable with who we are may just be the beginning. Many of us live and move every day inside of our family systems. Our parents, partners, children, and so many others make up those family systems, and living in a family means the identity of the family changes when the identity of one member of that family changes. Think about spin art, the classic kids' toy. One drop of paint onto a spinning canvas can change the whole complexity of the painting. This is where we find ourselves. As we stand tall in our Queer identity, we are now dropped into our family systems, where those family members will now have their own work of journeying in, letting in, and journeying out in order to fully embrace the new colors on the family canvas. We know who we are, and we now get the privilege of walking this journey with our family.

Reflection

Who Am I?

Reflect on who you are as a person beyond your sexuality and gender.

Write a list of all the parts of you that you've already come to discover.

> What do you enjoy?
> What are your passions?
> Where do you find purpose?

It's helpful to have this list handy or even share it with people to whom you are coming out as a reminder that you are who you've always been and you are more than your sexuality and gender, even though your coming out may be perceived as a big change.

6

The Family Journey In

From the youngest age, we are subject to society's expectations about gender and sexuality. As schoolchildren, we are separated by genders and questioned about crushes; in high school, we crown the king and queen of prom; and as young adults, we celebrate marriages with lavish weddings stacked with the groomsmen and bridesmaids at our side. As much as modern life is beginning to subvert these expectations, it is engrained in most of us that the "norm" is a heterosexual, cisgender, 2.5-child existence.

This is not only codified into our social structure; it is also sanctified by many religions. For many of us, our religious identity supersedes any questions of gender or sexual identity. There are pockets of major religions in which we are seeing the acceptance of the gender and sexual spectrum. However, by and large, the picture presented by most religious organizations is that of heterosexual love and what some call the "traditional" family, which belies the preference of our societal and religious systems toward gender and sexual cis/heteronormativity.

With that in mind, let us begin this section by saying that when a loved one lets us in on their identity or comes out to us, it will deeply affect our own sense of self and identity. The closer the relationship, the more likely we are to feel conflicting emotions. Many parents struggle with feelings of guilt or shame that they didn't see their child's identity sooner, while at the same time feeling the joy that their child can live as they are. These feelings become even more complex when the individual revealing their identity is a spouse or life partner. It is not uncommon for a spouse to feel betrayed and angry. At the same time, a spouse may feel grateful that the person they love can be fully themselves. It is important that we acknowledge the presence of these emotions and examine where they are coming from and why we feel them.

It is tempting to allow our emotions to rule us as we traverse this journey. Our many overwhelming emotions can compound and mix in ways that can cause us anguish if we're not aware of what is happening inside of ourselves. While the tendency can be to turn our feelings outward and either fight with or fawn over our loved one—more on these responses below—in truth, we have to slow down and own our own process of discovery. The best way forward is to continually center our loved one's story and separate our story from theirs. While our stories are intertwined, they are not the same. Just as we are not responsible for our loved one's identity, they are not responsible for ours. They cannot tell us who we are as much as we cannot tell them who they are.

This may sound like an easy task, but untangling ourselves from our loved ones, our culture, our religion, or our many systems of life can be tricky and gut-wrenching. This kind of extrapolation of self returns us to differentiation, and it is an

integral part of emotional maturity. Differentiation is the opposite of enmeshment. When we are unable to separate our values,
desires, preferences, and opinions from one another without
fear of major negative repercussions in our relationship, we run
the risk of enmeshment. However, when we are able to differ
in opinion, respect one another's differences, and own our own
story in relationship, we are working toward differentiation.

It bears repeating that differentiation allows you to be you,
while I am allowed to be me. This is often a difficult stance for
parents and spouses to take because our lives are so intricately
and necessarily intertwined with our loved one. As parents, it
is likely that we will see our child's identity as a reflection of us.
It is not uncommon for a parent to say, "What did I do?" as a
result of a child's coming out. The answer is *nothing*. Your child's
healthy sexual and/or gender identity has nothing to do with
anything you did or did not do. Their ability to express it may
depend on you but not their core identity. The same is true for
spouses. When Nia came out to Katie, it was easy for Katie to
believe that she had not been "woman enough" for Nia. It's easy
to let our minds run away with us and tell us there is a *why* that
we can control. It would make this process a whole lot easier, but
it's simply not true. Sexual and gender identities are not things
to be controlled; they are identities to be celebrated and loved.

As we move through the family journey, it is important that
we begin with owning ourselves. It is tempting to place all of
our emotions on our loved one, but this is unfair to them and
insincere for us. Our emotions are not for our loved ones to
sort out; they are ours to examine, hold, and process so that
we can engage with our loved one in a way that is honoring to
them and true to ourselves. This most likely will require the aid
of a therapist, and we highly recommend that every family

member experiencing overwhelming emotional conflict seek professional help. With that said, we hope you will take time to slow down and breathe through your honest reactions to your loved one's coming out and begin by acknowledging your emotional responses and accepting the beautiful reality of who your loved one truly is.

Identifying Feelings

In order to start from a place of sincerity with ourselves and our loved ones, we must first acknowledge our emotions. This is often difficult when we are thrown for a loop or feel broadsided by new information. If our loved one comes to us with a revelation about their gender or sexual identity that rings true or validates intuitions we've held, we may not feel the same sense of imbalance as if we had no indications about our loved one's true gender or sexuality. This feeling of instability may be heightened if we are part of a culture or belief system that condemns or denies these core identities. We may even experience extreme stress when a loved one lets us in or comes out to us. This may trigger our fight, flight, freeze, or fawn response. It is important to acknowledge if we are triggered and examine our responses.

Fight

When we are in fight mode, our defenses shoot up. We feel an immediate sense of defense and offense—a feeling of "us versus them" that demands a winner and a loser. Each family member's fight response will look extremely different depending on their personality. One manifestation of the fight response is a feeling of aggression that leads to verbal, emotional, and sometimes physical altercations.

However, not all aggression looks like rage. Passive aggression is also a part of the fight response, along with emotional manipulation and gaslighting. These actions are quieter but just as harmful to our relationships. It is important that we understand our tendencies to slip into passive aggression just as it is vital to guard against physical aggression.

Flight

Those with a flight response will often respond in the exact opposite manner of fight. We feel the need to escape the situation and sometimes pretend it never happened. We may attempt to ignore what is happening, or what has already happened, in order to maintain an internal homeostasis. An indicator that we are in flight would be an extreme sense of withdrawal. It is often difficult to engage someone who flees as the main goal of the response is to remove oneself from the situation. However, without communication and closeness in relationship, we cannot grow closer to one another.

Freeze

A freeze response produces a deep sense of being stuck. If those with a flight response can't get out fast enough, those who freeze can't find the door. This can come with physical symptoms such as trouble breathing or numbness. That numb feeling can also be emotional as those who freeze tend to shut down in order to be able to function in other areas. It is easy for those with a freeze response to get wrapped around the axle of a situation and be unable to think things through to find a solution or resolution. Those who freeze need reminders that they can move forward.

Fawn

A relative newcomer to the triggered response category is fawn—acting to try to please the other person to avoid conflict. For those of us who fawn, it can be very difficult to differentiate a natural emotional response of love and empathy from a triggered response of compulsively self-sacrificing for the needs of the other person. Because fawning tends to look so much like a loving response, it is important that we take time to examine ourselves and understand if our acts of love are coming from a place of truth where we can own our own story and affirm our loved one or a place of fear where our story is threatened by our loved one's revelation. Our motivations can often get tangled, but a key indicator that we are in a triggered state is that we are doing things that come at the steep price of our own well-being, both physically and emotionally. While fawning can look and feel good, it leaves us weary and overloaded, without enough love for ourselves. Therefore, we can become easily embittered and resentful.

Having a fight, flight, freeze, or fawn response is neither good nor bad; it simply is our body's way of keeping us safe when we feel threatened. When we are able to take a breath, step back from the immediate situation, and recognize we are having a response, we are more likely to be able to acknowledge our feelings and course correct, coming down from our trigger before engaging in behavior we wouldn't engage in when we are not in our triggered state.

At the end of this chapter, we will provide grounding exercises to help de-escalate our triggered responses. As always, if your responses are heightened and beyond your control, leading to panic attacks or thoughts of harming yourself or others, it is essential to seek professional help as soon as possible. If your responses are acute and immediate, please see the footnote for the National Suicide and Crisis Lifeline[1] and the National Domestic Abuse Hotline.[2]

Whether we find ourselves in triggered responses or not, we will all shift through emotions related to our loved one's gender or sexuality identity disclosure. It is important to give ourselves permission to feel what is coming up for us and honor those feelings. Meditation can often be a good place to begin. When we settle our bodies, we can allow our emotions to come to the surface. When we notice, without judgment, what we are feeling, we can begin to address the realities of our own journey.

The Feeling Wheel

During the years following Nia's letting Katie in and her coming out publicly, the Feeling Wheel rose in popularity, and Katie found it helpful as a guide for understanding the conflicting emotions swirling inside her. She printed out a copy and kept one at her desk at work for easy reference when things got especially elevated in her body.

The Feeling Wheel was designed by Gloria Willcox[3] and is a tool used to help people name their emotions. The wheel begins from the outer circles with many emotional descriptors such as *furious, bewildered, amused, satisfied, serene,* and *apathetic.* As we follow the spokes inward, we find a distilled version of the emotion (i.e., *angry, rejected, playful, hopeful, loving,* and *lonely*).

Then we work closer to the middle circle, which is home to six key emotions identified as *sad, mad, joyful, peaceful, scared,* and *powerful.* The inner six emotions are primary emotions; the outer two circles are secondary emotions with varying intensity. What the Feeling Wheel helps us to do is name our secondary emotions so that we can address our primary emotions.

For example, we may immediately be able to identify that we are bewildered. The Feeling Wheel then helps us say, "I am

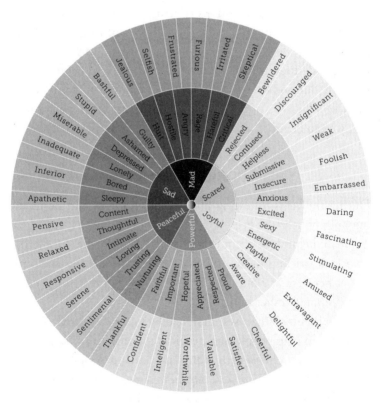

Figure 7: The Feeling Wheel (Transactional Analysis Journal, Taylor & Francis Ltd, http://www.tandfonline.com)

bewildered. I am bewildered because I am confused. I am confused because I am scared." This line of thinking helps us differentiate between "I'm fine" and "I'm not fine" by allowing us to state precisely what we are feeling so that we can accurately address our needs.

Taking the above example and applying it to a conversational situation with a loved one, saying "I am confused" can lead our loved one to feel as if they need to explain themselves further. In this case, *confused* focuses the emotion on the other person and demands an explanation, whereas when we drill down to understand that we are actually scared, we can own this emotion. Instead of coming at our loved one demanding an explanation, we are coming to our loved one expressing our feelings and asking for engagement. Hopefully, we will be met with kindness and understanding, and together we can begin to address our feelings.

Will there be times when our loved one is triggered by our emotional responses? Yes. Oh, yes! This is why it is important to recognize that we are all capable of feeling different things at the same time, and we are all responsible for owning our own emotions and not making others responsible for managing them. The important thing is to allow space for conflicting emotions and time to work through things on your own, with a therapist, and together as a family as you are able. Emotions are tricky little boogers; we all need patience when handling them.

Ambiguous Loss

Once our loved one comes out to us and we reach a place where we can acknowledge our feelings about what we are experiencing, conventional thought may tell us that we should be at a place of acceptance. While this would be terrific, it is not always the case; neither is it always fair.

Take, for instance, a child who just found out that their mother is a lesbian and their parents are divorcing amicably for the mother to pursue a new relationship with a woman. While the situation itself may be unfolding in a kind and generous way, the child is experiencing a loss. Their sense of stability may be shaken. Even in adulthood, that child is likely to feel a sense of grief as their world as they know it is changing. It would be a betrayal of that child to ask them to get over their feelings and find immediate acceptance of the situation, even if they did immediately accept their mother for who she is.

Psychologist Pauline Boss has done extensive work on a phenomenon she has dubbed *ambiguous loss*.[4] Boss defines ambiguous loss as a loss without closure. These losses can be difficult to define as such because they typically come with complicating circumstances. These may include a missing family member, a parent with dementia, an ongoing—perhaps fatal—illness, and so on. The two categories that Boss defines are losses in which the person is physically present but mentally/emotionally unavailable (i.e., dementia or mental illness) and when the person is mentally/emotionally present but physically unavailable (i.e., missing or in the military).

While Dr. Boss's research does not include gender transition, our experience leads us to believe that these life changes could be identified as ambiguous loss. We believe this kind of loss can also be broadened to anyone experiencing a gender or sexual awakening as the revelation of identity inherently houses both joy and pain.

When we can acknowledge the conflicting feelings that a loved one's coming out brings up in us, we can begin to name this as an ambiguous loss, which then opens the door for a very important step in the process of acceptance: grief. It can be scary and even might feel disrespectful to label our feelings as grief when our loved one comes out. However, by avoiding our grief, we are telling ourselves that part of our own journey is somehow bad or shameful. We are then harboring a secret grief that will inevitably eat away at our own freedom and joy.

It may be helpful to reframe grief as we seek to push into it, not as something to be avoided unless we experience catastrophic loss but rather as a natural part of the cycle of our lives. There's a reason people cry at graduations, weddings, births, and the like. These are happy tears, yes, but they are also tears of letting go, of moving on. They are tears of joy and of grief, and both belong.

In Katie's work as a birth doula, she has seen people cry for many reasons before delivery, during labor, and once the baby comes. In the singular act of giving life, there is so much pain, agony, ecstasy, joy, and humanity. We let go of one phase of our life and enter into a new phase. Our bodies know this; that's why we prepare in so many ways. Birth is filled with gains and losses—all of life is. The same is true for our loved one when they come out, and the same is true for us. We're beginning something new and maybe letting go of some things we've loved. It's okay to mourn. We don't have to understand all of grief, but we can accept that it is natural to grieve. We can give ourselves permission to feel, and in doing so, we allow an unshackling of ourselves from things that no longer serve us.

Forgiving Reality

Once we have acknowledged our grief and given ourselves time to honor our emotions, we still may find ourselves stuck, unable to move forward, unable to let go. For some, especially spouses and grown children, letting go of what has been and walking into what will be can be exceptionally difficult. When we feel at a loss, we often want to hold fast to what we know because the unknown can be so unnerving. When we find ourselves in this place, it is time for forgiveness.

Forgiveness may be a difficult concept for those of us brought up in specific religious or cultural contexts. For us, as Evangelical Christians, forgiveness was intricately tied to sin. Because the world sinned, Jesus had to be sent as a token of forgiveness. If we did something deemed "bad," we had to ask for forgiveness. Christian practices like communion, public or private confession, and others are designed as times for us to atone for our sins and ask forgiveness. You may have had similar practices in your religious or cultural background. We want to be clear: This is not the kind of forgiveness we are talking about. The forgiveness we are leading you to has no rights or wrongs. It is not primarily about sin. It is a movement toward acceptance.

Franciscan Father Richard Rohr became a large influence in our lives as we expanded our spiritual landscape during Nia's coming-out journey, so much so that Katie enrolled in and later was sent from his organization's Living School. During her time at the Living School, Katie was introduced to the idea of *forgiving reality*—a sort of radical acceptance of things as they are. It was particularly timely as Katie was participating in the school remotely because of the COVID-19 pandemic. During the course of her program, we experienced major world events such as the killing of George Floyd and the insurrection at the US Capitol on January 6, 2021. It seemed as if our world were falling apart collectively as well as privately as we navigated Nia's coming out.

We were all searching for answers, and the idea of forgiving reality seemed like a slap in the face. However, as we began to peel back the true meaning of forgiveness of reality, it became a source of great freedom. Forgiveness had always come with a forgetting that didn't seem helpful. If we forget what caused the need for forgiveness in the first place, we lose our ability to determine what is acceptable and unacceptable going forward.

On the contrary, forgiving reality allows us to look at what is happening right now and drop the labels of *good* and *bad*, instead saying "this is what it is." It is happening. It has happened. We stop trying to change past events that have caused us pain and instead acknowledge the pain and grief we are experiencing. We are able to open our eyes to our role and responsibility related to where we want to go next. We can formulate clear boundaries to help us not repeat harmful patterns in the areas that we can control and let go of the self-expectation that we should carry more of the blame or burden than is ours. The simplicity of forgiving reality can be found in the Serenity Prayer written by Reinhold Niebuhr and used in Alcoholics Anonymous: "God grant me the serenity to accept the things I cannot change, courage to change the things I can, and the wisdom to know the difference."

When viewed through this lens, forgiveness becomes an active process of letting go and leaning in appropriately. There are realities we can enter into and begin to change, and there are those things that have happened that we can't control. We don't have to forget. We don't have to be thankful. We don't have to like it. In fact, we can and sometimes should hate it. However, when we forgive reality, we realize the difference between what is ours to do and what is ours to let go of. We are granted the serenity to accept the things we cannot change and the courage to change the things we can.

A loved one's coming out may come with some difficult realities, both past and future. There will be emotions to navigate, relationships to reassess, and family dynamics to consider. When we come to this reality with an open hand instead of a closed fist, we are much more likely to make decisions that benefit each member of our inner circle. We are more able to step outside of our defenses and much more likely to find our common story. Freedom begins with a letting go of what was, an embrace of what is, and an active love for what will be. This is forgiveness.

Discovering Self

One of the more difficult things to do when a loved one comes out is to separate our experience from theirs. It is easy to settle all of our attention on their identity and their needs and avoid caring for and exploring our own needs and discovering aspects of our own identity that may be coming forward. However, in order to develop a healthy relationship dynamic, it is imperative that we know and own ourselves. Admittedly, this can be hard to do when something that has defined us—such as being the wife of a husband, the child of a mom and a dad, the parent of a girl, or one half of a pair of brothers—has seemingly, suddenly changed, and we have to reevaluate that identity.

This can be even more difficult when our loved one's Queer identity clashes with our cultural, racial, or religious identity. Throw in our vocational identity, our social identity, and our own sexual and gender identities, and it becomes evident that we don't live in a vacuum where we can quarantine one part of ourselves away from the others. Our identities are intersectional, and when we pull the string of one of those identities, as much as it seems like all will come crashing down, it gives us the opportunity to reassess and name much of who we are and who we want to be. This is one of the great gifts of a loved one's journey if we choose to walk beside them.

KATIE LEAN-IN: When Nia was transitioning, I often found myself deeply uncomfortable. One of these early discomforts was Nia's need to try on a lot of different outward expressions of her femininity through clothing. As Nia's wardrobe grew, I noticed myself feeling emotions of insecurity and jealousy I hadn't felt for many years. This was especially difficult when Nia would purchase an item of clothing that I already owned or something similar. It set off something in me that I wasn't used to, that I thought I had dealt with.

I had already made a commitment to myself to understand my discomfort before coming to Nia with it. So as Nia continued to buy more clothing, shoes, and accessories, I started listening to the difficult emotions rising up in me. Utilizing tools learned in therapy, I sought the source of my feelings by thinking through the first time I remembered feeling this way. Slowly, things started to reveal themselves.

As an adolescent, I was extremely self-expressive. I wore polyester leisure suits I had found at garage sales and clear platform silver wingtips. I experimented with my hair and my accessories. In short, I was a carefree kid living out my fashion dreams without any sort of self-consciousness. I was as thirteen as a thirteen-year-old girl in the '90s could be.

However, this penchant for far-out fashion did not go unnoticed. Kids at school commented, my sisters begged me to wear something normal, and although she was very supportive,

I was often compared to my stylish and beautiful mom. As an awkward thirteen-year-old with a wacky look, there was no way to not internalize the idea that something about my style was wrong. So eventually I started to tone myself down. I still wore interesting clothing and threw in an accessory now and then that I felt really strongly about, but by the time I was in college, I found myself lamenting a version of myself I had let go of in order to fit in just a little better.

Realizing this made me sad. I'm still uncovering the parts of me that I gave up in order to satisfy a cultural norm that I had internalized. I had tried, and often failed, to dilute myself enough to fit in while still standing out just enough to be noticed. Now Nia was experimenting with all the things I loved when I was thirteen, and my body was telling me that she was going to get hurt if she allowed herself to love the things she really loved, and I was going to get hurt if she took any of the individuality that I had carefully squirreled away for myself. I realized I had curated an outward identity of a person I thought I was supposed to be.

Once I began understanding this reality, I started to make changes in the way I presented myself to the world. I almost immediately cut my shoulder-length blond hair into a close-cropped pixie and shortly thereafter dyed it purple. I got a tattoo, and then another, and then another. I had always been afraid of buying quality clothing because my tastes changed so quickly. When I realized this was because I was trying to live out my idea of someone else's style, it was easier to buy pieces I loved that were quirky simply because I liked them and felt good in them.

Of course, this issue goes deeper than clothing. I had always felt my personality was too big and had been told so more than a few times. The great gift of Nia's coming out was that I was able to assess for myself if this was true. If I really was too much. If my loud personality, which matched my loud look, was unacceptable. There are still parts of me I'm trying to dislodge from a lifetime of being pushed down. However, I realize now that I get to be who I am, and no one else can tell me if that is good or not. I have to be satisfied with myself. I'm learning to do that.

This is also very important for our Queer loved one to understand. Their identity does affect our identity, especially if they overlap in intimate ways, such as with a spouse. Queer folks who are aware of this dynamic can make space for what we are going through as well. This is where differentiation becomes such an incredibly vital part of our journeys. Our Queer loved one should have the freedom to explore and own their identity, and family members should have the same freedom. There are times when this exploration should overlap, and there are times when we will have to do some hard work on our own, with a therapist, or with a trusted ally.

Finding Our North Star

Finding ourselves is deceptively complex. After all, we live with ourselves day in and day out, so we ought to know ourselves quite well, right? However, if we look closely, many of us may find that what we really know about ourselves is our reactions, not necessarily the truth of who we are. This is why we encourage so much work on identifying emotions, naming them, and understanding what we are feeling. Often, our reactions can get in the way of our deeper responses that are aligned with our true nature. Our true nature comes out when we are able to dig past our reactions and find our responses. This becomes easier when we find our North Star, that deepest desire that can guide us through our lives.

Just like Peter Pan always knew how to get back home to Neverland by following the second star to the right, we, too, can orient ourselves to our true self by understanding our North Star. When we dig into our real desires for our life and let what we love lead us to the center of ourselves, it becomes easier to identify how we want to respond to any given situation based on the North Star we've anchored ourselves to. We can ask ourselves, "Will this action bring me closer to my North Star or push me farther from it?"

One afternoon after Nia's disclosure, while running countless errands, Katie turned on *The Rob Cast*, a podcast by a popular progressive Christian teacher, Rob Bell. He was workshopping ideas for a new book and began discussing desire. Katie can't remember much about exactly what was said during this podcast, but one thing did stand out. Bell mentioned the idea that our deepest desires are God-given signposts to our true nature. He kicked around the idea of challenging the concept that our desires are evil and invited listeners to consider the idea of embracing our desires as a map back to ourselves.

Katie took the opportunity, on the gravel road back home, to really contemplate her desires for her life. It was clear to her that what she truly wanted wasn't specifically a husband or a father for her children. What Katie wanted was a partner with whom to build an authentic life filled with love, where each member of her family was free to be completely themselves. It was clear to her that this was what she had with Nia, and the thought of giving that up was an impossible one. Katie was able to clarify in that moment that her North Star was not in conflict with her reality.

From this jumping-off point, a clarity came over decisions that would continue to crop up. As we were confronted with the loss of friends, family, and community, it would have been easy for Katie to buckle under the pressure to feel slighted or even betrayed by Nia's coming out. However, because Katie had a firm anchor to her North Star, she was able to constantly remind herself that she had the agency to do what she wanted and needed as Nia continued in her transition. By establishing her North Star, Katie prevented a victim mentality and assumed agency inside of Nia's blossoming identity and her own.

Being anchored to a North Star also helps us to identify those who will support us through the letting-in and coming-out processes. When we can firmly live in our deepest desire and express it to others, our declarations should not be met with argument or pushback but with support and love. There were many times when a friend or acquaintance would ask if we were staying together through Nia's transition. Those who were good supporters accepted our yes the first time. Incredible supporters, those we would call *accomplices* later on and *friends* always, never even had to ask. They already knew Katie's North Star because they lived alongside her, watching her love Nia and watching Nia love her.

When we know ourselves, we can trust ourselves. Establishing a North Star is one way we can build trust in ourselves because we have something to come back to. We are no longer wandering aimlessly. We are on a path to somewhere. We know where home is, and we can always find our way back, even if the night is dark. We can feel it.

Embracing Our True Ethic

Another vital part of knowing ourselves and trusting ourselves is knowing our *true ethic*. That is the way in which we walk in the world because of what we believe. True ethic is closely associated with our ideologies; it is what we believe about the world. It's the fuel for our actions and passions. For some of us this ethic springs from religious or spiritual origins. It doesn't have to, but we have found it is usually heavily influenced by the culture in which we were raised. When our ethic is wrapped in culture or religion, it might take some time to tease out exactly what we believe and how we will apply it to our lives. Finding our true ethic requires us to ask ourselves difficult questions of why we believe what we believe and what is truly at the root of it all.

When Nia let Katie in on her identity, we had already been exploring what our true ethic was, both together and separately. Our religious upbringings had introduced us to many spiritual ideas, and through our lifetimes, we had been sifting through what resonated with us and what didn't. Both of us had reached a point in our spiritual journeys where we had come to understand love as our supreme ethic. Having grown up in the Christian tradition, our example of Godlike love was Jesus.

We pored over stories of Jesus and his responses to people. Always, Jesus responded to people in love. Those labeled prostitutes, heretics, demoniacs, and whores were accepted, loved, and empowered by Jesus. In fact, Jesus reserved his harshest criticism for those who wielded their power, both political and religious, over others to push them into lives of submission through guilt and shame. It seemed to us that Jesus lived a radical life driven by the ethic of love that refused to shame people and also held those in power to account. This is the ethic we were exploring when Nia came out. Nia had found that God loved her exactly as she was, and she could live free from fear and shame. In short, Nia's true ethic is that love sees us and desires to help us become our complete selves.

Katie also studied this ethic and expanded her understanding, reaching a place that has allowed her to accept that not all love leads to closeness. Love that mutually respects and honors is the guiding ethic of Katie's life. This has sometimes led to pain as respectful, honoring love sometimes means boundaries have to be drawn. By and large, this ethic of mutually honoring and respectful love has allowed Katie to acknowledge her reactions, honor her emotions, and respond to others in ways that honor her commitment to her life ethic.

Finding our life's ethic may seem like an insurmountable task. However, truly, what we are searching for is inside of us. What we must do is listen and ask ourselves the question: What do we want our life to look like? Beyond labels, beyond circumstances. When all else is stripped away, what do we want to guide us at the end of the day? This will be different for each of us. Boundaried love is Katie's ethic. We can't tell you what yours should be or is. Only you can define how you want to live in this world.

Process over Perfection

There is no way we can address every issue that will come up once your loved one comes out. Everyone's circumstances and family structures are unique, and each family will experience this journey of identity in different ways. What we do know for sure is that none of us is perfect. There aren't many people who have gotten to the other side of their coming out and said, "Well that went exactly as I would have hoped." We still haven't met anyone who's expressed that sentiment to us.

It is far more realistic that each of us will, at some point during our journey, feel out of our depth. We will make mistakes. We will use the wrong pronouns, we will remember how homophobic our language used to be, and we will struggle with things we think should be easy. When we feel this way, we tend to do one of two things: become defensive or give up. That is why we want to be clear that we will all mess up. We will all do this wrong at some points, but if we are willing to admit our mistakes and learn from them, we will grow as individuals and as families.

The most powerful words we can say to each other are *I'm sorry*. When we let go of our need to perfectly walk this road without any mistakes, we realize that we are all human beings learning to be the best versions of ourselves. Sometimes we will need to make amends for glaring errors. Other times, we will have to apologize for actions we took or things we said when we thought we were right. These are hard things to do, but they are necessary—both for our personal growth and for the health of our relationships.

In our house, we have learned to love the phrase *process over perfection*. It reminds us that there is no perfect anything. If that were the case, we could just write a book giving you clear outlines of how to love each other without fault. We can't do that. No one can. However, what we can tell you is that when we embrace the process of becoming who we are, lumps and all, we are kinder, more generous, and more forgiving with ourselves and each other. This is what love is—sticking with each other through the process.

Reflection

Identifying Feelings

* Can you identify your trigger response; fight, flight, freeze, and/or fawn?
  * How do you know when you are acting out of a triggered response?
  * In what ways do you respond when you are triggered?
  * What are some ways you can find the distance in order to come down from your trigger and find your true emotion and response?
  * What mode of response is more in line with your values, and how can you recognize when you are responding in your preferred way?
* Take some time to familiarize yourself with the Feeling Wheel above. When you are feeling a strong emotion, ask yourself the following questions:
  * What is the immediate feeling I can name?
  * What is the circumstance that led to that feeling?
  * Is there a deeper emotion associated with the feeling I am experiencing?
  * When have I felt this feeling before?
  * What is the core emotion I am experiencing?
  * What do I need to acknowledge the root emotion I am experiencing and not try to run away from it?

○ How do I care for myself and find support as I hold this emotion and work through my feelings?

Exercises

5-4-3-2-1 Grounding

When we find ourselves in a triggered or panicked state, it can be difficult to regain control. One of the most effective ways to find equilibrium is connecting with our bodies. The 5-4-3-2-1 method allows us to move from our head-centered cycle into a body-centered grounding experience. When you find yourself having trouble taking control of your emotions or thoughts, try the following:

Find a safe, comfortable area to sit yourself in a relaxed position. Take three deep breaths in.

5: Identify five things in the room you can see. Describe them either out loud or internally. Take time to really see them.

4: Identify four things you can touch around you. This may be your feet on the floor or your back against the chair. Notice how your skin feels and what it is like to be in your body.

3: Identify three sounds you can hear. Pay careful attention to the whooshing of the air or the ticking of the clock. Give yourself permission to feel your ears listening to your environment.

2: Identify two odors you can smell. You may have lit a candle to start this meditation, or perhaps dinner is cooking. This may be as simple as smelling your own laundry detergent or your pet's fur. Take time to fully inhale and exhale.

1: Identify one thing you can taste. Sometimes the hardest of all, identifying something you taste is the final step in the 5-4-3-2-1 method. Bring awareness to your mouth and tongue and try to identify what you are tasting.

At the conclusion of this exercise, breathe in three more deep breaths and allow yourself a moment to come back to the reality of the room around you. Try to carry your body awareness with you as you move forward with your day.

Who Am I?

Take some time to meditate, clear your mind, and journal through the questions below. Come back to these often and truly challenge yourself to answer honestly. You may want to share this exercise with a trusted friend or partner.

* Who am I?
* What do I assume about myself?
* What needs to be challenged?
* Is there a freer version of me?
* How do I find me?

North Star / True Ethic Meditation

For one week, take five minutes every day to sit in quiet meditation and reflect on the following:

* What is most important to me in life?
* How do I see myself in the world?

* What do I believe is the highest virtue? Who is an example of that virtue to me?
* What guides me in my life?

After five days, set a timer and journal for ten minutes. What comes forward for you? Can you name an ethic you would like to own? If not, can you name why? Continue this exercise or revisit it when you feel you've lost your anchor to your life's ethos.

7

The Family Journey of Letting Others In

Hopefully, after starting the process of exploring our own emotions and identity, we have begun to build a good base for letting others in on our family journey. Feeling hesitant about letting others in is natural. While the process looks different for each family, it is an important part of our growth. You should never feel pressure to let others in, but you should recognize the signs that you may benefit from more support. Some of these signs include a feeling of overwhelm that doesn't subside, difficulty performing daily tasks without dwelling on your family situation, and physical symptoms such as panic attacks or a feeling of emotional or physical numbness.

These are all signs that our bodies and minds just cannot bear the weight of what we are dealing with alone. It is imperative that you seek support as soon as possible if any of these signs have become your reality. If you do not have trusted allies in your life, make it a priority to see your doctor or seek a therapist. Often we will need the help of professionals to move our way through the realities of embracing a Queer loved one. The feeling of relief is amazing when we simply open ourselves to trusted loved ones and allow them into what is happening in our lives.

As previously discussed, our journey is linked with our loved ones but is also intimately our own. We will have thoughts and feelings that need to be addressed outside of the relationship with our loved one in order to protect them and our relationship with them. We may need to vent and ask for advice. We may need to cry and grieve with someone who can understand what we are going through without feeling personally responsible for our emotions. Sometimes we will need things that our loved one can't or should not be responsible for. Letting others in allows us the safety of trusted relationships as we navigate our loved one's disclosure.

Identifying Individual Circles of Safety

Once we decide we are ready to start letting people in, we may also find ourselves revisiting our personal journey as new perspectives tend to bring up new emotions. This is why being able to trust those we are letting in is so important. Earlier we spoke about circles of safety as connected to our loved one—the inner circle of stars within the circle of support. Now we need to also think of our own circles of safety where we are the centered individual. When we visually represent our own centering, we give ourselves permission to focus on our needs.

It is important to note that while each individual can have their own circles of safety independent from others, there are points at which our circles will begin to overlap and become a Venn diagram, where who I am and what I need meet who you are and what you need. That is what it means to be in relationship.

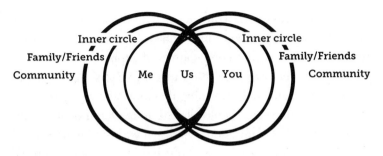

Figure 8: Where Your Circles Meet Mine

The overlap in the diagrams is where we work together taking both of our needs and our identities into account. However, we cannot do this effectively if we don't know ourselves or our needs. If we don't know ourselves, eventually one half of the Venn diagram will push the other out, and we will either become completely enmeshed in our loved one's identity, or we will reject their identity as wholly incompatible with our own. This is why finding our own sources of support is so vital. Without this sense of differentiation, we will eventually lose sight of our own perspective. If we can maintain autonomy throughout our loved one's journey, we can embark on our own journey and discover new and wonderful things about ourselves. This will hopefully strengthen our relationship with our loved one and others.

As we begin to consider who may be in our circles of safety, we suggest starting with a commitment to affirming sources of support. We emphasize affirming support because it is vitally important to be cared for by those who see our loved ones as beautiful and whole. If we have chosen to accept our loved ones and are committed to relationship with them, we must honor their identity by placing it in the hands of those who will treat it with tenderness.

We know this can be a difficult step for those of us who come from nonaffirming backgrounds and don't know who to trust. We can assure you that good sources of support will not push you beyond where you are ready to go. Doctors are trained to remain nonjudgmental. Affirming therapists and clergy may ask revealing questions but should allow us to reach our own conclusions. Reputable organizations will listen without judgment and provide resources when we are struggling. If we are going to be loving supports for our loved ones, we must start with affirmation of who they are. Good sources of support will also acknowledge our journey and feelings. Those who provide good support are there to help us find our way, not push their opinions onto us. We stress affirming care because those who already affirm our loved one's identity can help give us the perspective we may not already have and help us meet our questions and struggles with compassion, both for ourselves and our loved ones.

As we consider who may come into our circles of support during the letting-in process, here are some criteria to consider:

* Does this person/organization affirm my loved one's identity?
* Can this person be supportive of me without becoming angry with my loved one or me?
* Is this person/organization trustworthy and confidential?
* Do I respect advice/counsel from this person/organization?
* Can this person/organization attend to my needs without making it about themselves?

We may find that we have to look beyond the structures of support already in place in our lives to find supports that fit this criterion. Initial safety may come in any one of the concentric circles of our lives. We may find that our close family members cannot handle the disclosure of our loved one's gender or sexual identity or that it is unsafe to let members of our religious community into our processing. This is when it becomes important to look at the resources available in our community or larger spiritual landscape. Perhaps we know of an affirming congregation within our religious tradition and are able to reach out to clergy for advice. Teens who are wrestling with the disclosure of a loved one may find support at school through organizations like the Genders and Sexualities Alliance (GSA) Network or a trusted affirming teacher. Parents and spouses can access PFLAG through its national website, pflag.com, for resources.

A growing stream of resources is opening up on the internet for people who are searching for help. Our own organization, Love in the Face (loveintheface.com), supports LGBTQ+ identifying individuals, their families, and communities. We also recommend a terrific organization called Transmission Ministry Collective (transmissionministry.com) working with trans individuals and their communities in matters of faith. We highly encourage looking through our resource page at the back of the book to find an organization that can help you in confidence. If choosing to explore other resources, look for the "About" or "What We Believe" section of an organization's website to ensure that values align.

Beyond affirming organizations, we also encourage seeking those individuals who give off hints that they are or would be affirming. It can be scary to broach the subject of a loved one's Queer identity, but some signs that someone can be trusted are:

* They have publicly affirmed Queer individuals in the past.
* They have a Queer loved one with whom they have a good relationship.

* They themselves are Queer, out, and proud.
* They have affirming paraphernalia, such as a Pride sticker or pronoun pin.

It may be difficult to identify affirming individuals if we do not inhabit affirming spaces. If this is the case, we suggest finding those spaces and taking the leap to reach out. A low-stakes way to begin is by attending a Pride event, which is usually celebrated in June in most US states. For those unfamiliar with Pride, this can seem like a daunting endeavor. Our cultural context may have painted a misleading picture for us of Pride parades that highlights debauchery and depraved behavior. In fact, many Pride celebrations have events that are tailored to families, and many religious communities offer events during this time as well. Finding a Pride event geared toward families or others inside our value system can connect us with other people in our same life stage facing the same struggles.

We also suggest looking into support groups around your area. When Nia came out, her local gender clinic had just begun offering a support group for trans individuals and allies. The support we received from this small, fledgling group of people was immense. While Nia had a growing community of support from other trans folks, for Katie, going to this group was the first time she had ever been in a group of trans individuals. It helped her feel more regulated about her experience and less alone. We became friends with several members of the group and ended up hosting a few of our new friends at our regular open-house-style Easter with our community and family members. This group helped us put our feet back on the ground when we felt unmoored and showed us that we could indeed build a beautiful and diverse community. It lessened our fear and broadened our scope of what could be. Not every support group is right for every person, and we highly suggest vetting any organization before jumping right in. However, a good organization with good facilitators can help us orient ourselves properly instead of spinning out of control with nowhere to land.

Our strongest suggestion is, of course, to find a licensed, affirming therapist. It is imperative that we have good mental healthcare. In addition, we may find that we need a medical doctor as well to help us assess if we need any medical care as we walk this journey with our loved one. For Katie, the compounding stress of Nia's disclosure plus a history of depression and anxiety hit its peak when Nia came out publicly and then the COVID-19 pandemic hit. After battling with multiple daily panic attacks and suicidal ideation, Katie decided it was time to see her medical doctor and ask for help. Walking into the office and sitting on the edge of the table, her doctor took one look at her and compassionately said, "Let's get you some help." They quickly began the process of getting Katie on psychiatric medication. For the first time in months, Katie wept. In that doctor's office, she experienced the compassionate care that she had been longing for from an impartial, nonjudgmental source who was there for only her in that moment. Of course, medication didn't solve everything, but it did help clear the cobwebs and allowed Katie to operate on a less triggered level throughout her day-to-day life. It goes without saying, but we will say it anyway just to clear up any confusion: mental healthcare is the number one support we should give to ourselves, and we should do it as soon as humanly possible.

When you have begun to identify a few individuals or organizations, fill them out in your circles of safety at the end of the chapter. Refer back often and make changes as necessary. Once you have established whom you would like to be in your circles, take time to discuss disclosure with your loved one.

Getting on the Same Page

As we begin to feel ready to let others in, remember that there is only one person in the driver's seat, and that is our Queer loved one. It can be tempting to convince ourselves that what we are going through belongs solely to us and is separate from our loved one, so much so that we may end up acting as if to whom and when we disclose their identity, even in seeking support, is up to us. This could not be further from the truth. Your loved one's identity belongs to them, and when we share who they are without their consent, we are betraying our relationship with them.

A good way of thinking about how we should treat disclosure and support-seeking is to consider our loved one's gender or sexuality as we would a pregnancy or birth announcement. Unless we have very skewed boundaries, most of us would concede that announcing a pregnancy or birth of a baby is up to the parent(s) of that child. Few of us would share with friends, family, or—God forbid—social media the birth of a child who isn't ours without the consent of their parent(s). Even when we are discussing grandchildren or nieces and nephews, most of us can agree that it is not our place as grandparents or aunts and uncles to make birth announcements without permission. The same is true for our loved one's gender or sexual identity. Our experience is our own, but their identity does not belong to us. Therefore, they deserve the right to control the disclosure of that information.

In the event that our loved one has come out publicly while we are still in the letting-in phase, navigating whom to let into our experience becomes somewhat clearer and more defined. In this case, the question is no longer "Whom should I let in?" but "Whom shouldn't I let in?" We encourage those who come out and who are ready to be known to make that explicit in their conversations with loved ones.

If your loved one hasn't made that clear to you, have a discussion with them. Something as simple as saying, "I know you came out publicly, but I want to make sure it's okay that I discuss your coming out with others. Is there anyone you don't want me discussing this with?" The simple act of asking goes a long way toward building trust in our relationships and showing our loved ones we care. We may also be surprised to learn that even though our loved one is officially out, there are still people or communities they don't wish to have knowledge of their disclosure. There are many reasons this may be the case. We don't always need to know why. We simply need to know.

If our loved one is still in the letting-in phase of their journey, it is our duty to know exactly whom it is appropriate to let in. If our loved one is our child or our spouse, it is incredibly important to be in continual conversation about whom to let in and when. As with any other life event, consent for disclosure is a must. Without this base of trust and mutual respect, disclosure can begin to feel like a game of telephone beyond the control of those whom it affects the most.

When Katie was ready to let someone in on her own for the first time, it snuck up on her. As Katie was on the way out the door to meet a friend, Nia said, "If you feel like you need to tell Keri about me, you can." Katie replied, "I won't." However, this was the first time the idea of spontaneously letting someone in came up in her mind. Nia had given Katie permission to let someone in, but Katie really didn't think anything would come up to naturally let our friend in on Nia's transgender identity.

While sitting al fresco with amazing wine and cheese, talking and laughing later that night, Keri mentioned what a great dresser Nia was. She commented specifically on the androgynous way that Nia had started dressing and how much she loved the pink jeans Nia wore to church the last week. She was so effusive about how great Nia's style was that Katie could not ignore the opportunity. Thanking her lucky stars that Nia had floated the idea of letting Keri in on Nia's gender journey, Katie took a deep breath and said, "Well, her style is so good because Nia is transgender."

Even now, when Katie remembers this moment, she can palpably recall the way the air stood still for just the tiniest second. Keri, so amazingly, drew in a breath and made the disclosure of Nia's identity seem like a natural and good thing. It was clear that there was a long road ahead, but she committed herself to walking it with us. She asked permission to tell her husband, also a good friend, and they became two of the first people, besides Katie's younger sister, Sami, who affirmed Nia and could also focus their support around Katie and what she was experiencing. This was a relief for both of us because Katie was no longer isolated in her processing and had encouraging supports to lean on.

The relief was immense. Letting someone else in eased the burden of all we were keeping within the walls of our house. Someone else knew and could support Katie as she navigated the journey ahead. When we surprised guests at our going-away party from Iowa with a vow renewal ceremony, this friend screamed, "I knew it!" She knew how to support us then, and she still knows now.

Had Nia not given permission to Katie to let Keri in on her identity, this story would probably have a very different ending. Disclosing without Nia's permission, and then perhaps asking

Keri to hide this knowledge from Nia, would have been a disaster, creating more angst for Katie. In turn, having Nia discover that Katie had betrayed her trust would have wounded our relationship. Being open and honest about our needs and keeping lines of communication open about whom we are communicating with are essential to grow trust in our relationships, both with our loved one and those who support us.

It is imperative that we take time to consult with our loved ones on whom can be let in. If we are not in ongoing daily communication with our loved one, we can ask them if they are willing to sit down with us for fifteen minutes or so to talk about letting others in. We need to be clear with them that this conversation is to understand their comfort level with us letting others in and that we simply need support. In many cases, our loved ones would jump at the opportunity to make sure we're supported. They may have great ideas on where we should go or whom we should talk to. If we know whom we would like to let in, we can specifically name those people and why they are trustworthy as we talk to our loved one. Be as specific as possible in order to allay any fears.

It is important to note that our loved ones may push back, especially if they are leery of someone's reaction to their identity. If they are adamant that we not let that specific person in, we can ask to revisit disclosure to that person at another time. If we truly believe that someone we want to let in will be a trustworthy support, we should explain that carefully and thoughtfully. If they still refuse, we need to respect their decision and offer an alternative or ask whom they are comfortable with us speaking to.

In the early stages, some loved ones may not be ready to let anyone else in. If this is the case and you know you need mental health support for your own well-being, let your loved one know lovingly that you will be seeking an LGBTQIA+-affirming doctor, -therapist, and/or -organization who will confidentially support you. You can also ask them which organizations may be helpful or let them know that you will be attending confidential support groups from trusted LGBTQIA+ allies. This is one example of how self-differentiation and boundaries come into play in relationships.

There is a big difference between social support and mental health support, and as long as you know that you will be given affirming support and your time together will be kept confidential, finding mental health support is your decision and not something your loved one can dictate. We suggest a doctor, therapist, or LGBTQIA+-affirming organization because they are ethically bound to confidentiality.

Creating a Timeline

For those of us who find ourselves with conflicting opinions of whom to let in, we find it helpful to walk through a loose timeline together with our loved one. *Timeline* is an imperfect word as it denotes a specific sequence of events in a specific time period, but what we are really talking about here is a series of if/then realities that allow for change and redirection but also allow us to come to a rough understanding of each other's needs. When we work together to create a timeline for letting in, we open the discussion and hope that each of our needs will be met. Even though our loved one is in the driver's seat of their identity, it is still important for us to gently voice how we are affected and what kinds of support we need. We all deserve to have our needs met.

In the Exercise section at the end of this chapter, you will find a timeline worksheet. We encourage you to sit down with your loved one and think about what each of you needs during the letting-in process and what you are comfortable with. You may not agree on the timing of every disclosure, but using if/ then scenarios may be helpful, such as, "I don't want your mom to know about my gender identity right now. However, if I come to a point where I feel more comfortable in my own skin and you feel confident enforcing boundaries with her, we can discuss if it feels safe for both of us to let her in." This is not always a perfect solution and can be a difficult conversation. We encourage coming back to a place of compassion toward ourselves and each other and finding common ground. Often the solution to these difficult quandaries is making sure we have clear boundaries with ourselves, each other, and those we let in.

Safety versus Comfort

There will be many times throughout our journey with our loved one when we feel discomfort. There are many times emotions may arise in us that we don't like. This is true for those we are vetting for our circles of support as well. Because many of us may not have encountered affirming spaces before, we may feel out of our depth or self-conscious in these spaces. We may even feel the twinges of disgust or self-righteousness. This is why we emphasize understanding our emotions and observing them closely. Our discomfort should be acknowledged and explored. However, in most cases, it should not preclude us from entering these spaces unless our discomfort in turn makes us an unsafe presence in those spaces because we are unable to keep our opinions, feelings, and judgments to ourselves. If we are able to enter uncomfortable scenarios with an open heart and a nonjudgmental attitude, we should push ourselves to find spaces that challenge us.

Safety, however, is an entirely different ball of wax. Feeling unsafe in a situation or relationship is a key indicator that it is time to get out of Dodge, at least for a while. Levels of safety vary for each individual person, so it is important to understand what wounds us and what we will not tolerate. Of course, physical violence or intimidation is usually the easiest form of unsafe environment to spot and should be addressed immediately in the form of leaving that situation.

More difficult-to-understand forms of unsafety are emotionally, mentally, and spiritually threatening situations. Depending on where we are in our journey, these emotional, mental, and spiritual safety points may be different. However, some key markers of safety should be followed. Sometimes it's easier to identify safe spaces if we know what unsafe situations look like. These may include:

* Bullying, including name-calling, emotional manipulation, violence, or threats of violence, based on your loved one's identity or your support of your loved one.
* Refusal to acknowledge your loved one's identity, including pronouns and name.
* Refusal to include your loved one's significant other in events.
* Coercive spiritual practices such as conversion therapy or the labeling of support as *evil* or *demonic*.
* The inability of an individual or organization to respect your boundaries.
* Constant applied pressure without support that causes you physical, emotional, or spiritual distress.

When we were navigating Nia's experience, we found that as we opened up to certain people, they gave lip service to Nia's identity. However, these people refused to change her name and pronouns. Under the guise of trying to change, which is real and takes time, individuals were consistently using the wrong name and pronoun, refusing to apologize for their misstep, and becoming hostile when either one of us asked them to correct themselves. Proper pronoun usage and naming became a barometer for if a relationship was going forward in safety or if it was time to distance ourselves from the relationship.

This is just one example of the ways in which people believe they are being helpful or in some way saving us from ourselves but are indeed causing us pain. There is room for discomfort. In this example, there is room for missteps with new names and pronouns, but refusal to admit their mistake or apologize while consistently using incorrect monikers belies an unwillingness to enter what should be a mutual relationship of respect. As with whom to let in, sussing out unsafe situations becomes easier when we commit to setting and maintaining strict boundaries.

Setting Boundaries

Setting boundaries around ourselves is an essential step to staying healthy throughout our journey with our loved one. Just because we let people in doesn't mean they have complete access to us or to our loved one's identity. Boundaries are important to have because people don't always react, or continue reacting, in ways that are beneficial to us or them.

Founder of the Embodiment Institute, Prentis Hemphill (all pronouns) tells us, "Boundaries are the distance at which I can love you and me simultaneously."[1] By this logic, all relationships need boundaries. No matter what type of relationship we are in, it is healthy and good to establish what is and is not acceptable inside of that relationship. In this way, we build bridges toward each other and have appropriate gates that control the access to those bridges.

Each of us has a limited amount of energy inside of us. There is only so much we can give out in a day and also receive. Our emotions are directly tied to our energy levels, and when they are out of whack, we can revert to our triggered patterns. Creating boundaries protects our energy and helps our bodies and minds stay in a place of health and wholeness, making it easier to navigate our lives in accordance with our true ethic.

When considering boundaries, we need to ask ourselves some questions about our relationships. These may include:

* Do I feel energized and loved by this person or depleted and shameful around them?
* Can I trust this person to take my feelings and life experiences into consideration when interacting with me?
* Does this person treat me with dignity and respect?
* Would I treat someone the way this person treats me?
* What does this person bring into my life?
* Do I want what this person is offering me?

Boundaries should not be about whether or not people agree with us but how they approach conversation and how they treat us. Someone who bullies or denigrates us steals our energy. If it's clear that someone is not interested in listening to our point of view or honoring our experiences, then it may be time to enforce some boundaries about the way they interact with us.

Setting boundaries can look different for each person. Katie's way of understanding her own boundaries is thinking of her inner life as her home. Anyone who wants access to her energy comes to her door. This door has a knob, a lock, and keys, which Katie has control over.

Before Nia's transition, there was no door on Katie's inner home. People were allowed to go in and out anytime they wished. If someone called, she answered. If a person wanted to come over, she let them in. If anyone needed anything from her, she gave it. This left her completely drained of energy and pumped full of other people's opinions, needs, and thoughts. There was no room left for her and what she needed. At her most vulnerable, she couldn't take it anymore. She put up thick walls, kicked everyone out, and barred the door. No one was allowed in. She lived life behind a thick shield, finally safe but very alone.

Through a lot of work both spiritually and with her therapist, Katie realized that keeping the door barred kept her safe, but it also cut off her connection to the world. At some point, she was going to have to learn to open up the door again. She was going to have to allow appropriate access to others if she wanted a robust life.

Katie's boundaries became very clear to her, and eventually she was able, as individuals approached her for relationships, to ask herself if these people were trustworthy. For those with whom she had been in a previous relationship and had shut out, she had to test the waters. For some, the door needed to remain closed because it was clear the dynamic had not changed. For many, it was time to try again and open up appropriately. The last category of people were those she reached out to who could not agree to mutually appropriate boundaries and even crossed the ones clearly stated. These are still difficult relationships to live without—those whom we wish we had but are unable to be in relationship with because we hurt each other when in proximity to one another. However, now Katie knows when someone is honoring her and when they aren't. She can now live more fully into her life ethic, honoring herself and others and respecting how both she and they need to be loved.

When we get clear on our boundaries, it is important that we let people know what those boundaries are. Letting others know that we will not allow ourselves to participate in harmful patterns of behavior is one of the first steps in building new relationships grounded on mutual trust and respect. This may mean we need to tell our mother that if she continues calling to bad mouth our spouse, we will have to stop answering her calls. We may need to tell our Bible study leader that if they continue to dead name our daughter, we will not feel comfortable attending study. The most important element of boundary-setting is deciding what we will do when people do cross the line, such as not answering our phone, blocking someone's number, or finding a new study group that honors our wishes and who our child is.

Creating and keeping emotional boundaries is not an easy task. Honoring ourselves is the beginning of establishing healthy relationships. Communicating our needs and telling people how we feel after we've evaluated our emotions and understood our reactions help us to grow into more autonomous, self-possessed individuals. We cannot control people's reactions or behaviors, but we can control how we respond. Boundaries help us do this by providing a clear demarcation of what is and isn't acceptable to us in a relationship. When you are building your circle of support, it is important that your support system honors your boundaries and helps you hold them up when the going gets tough. That's why you need them. That's what you are asking from them.

Widening Circles

There is a gorgeous song by Rising Appalachia called "Wider Circles" that calls us into the work of making space by supporting one another. This song became a litmus test of sorts for Katie as she sought people whom she could trust through her journey as it encapsulates what she is looking for in a safe place of refuge and support. The song speaks of a mutual nature in relationship that guides, rejoices, joins, holds, and acts with love and energy. These kinds of relationships do something very important in our world. They make space. They widen our circles because there is room for everyone.

As a society, we often mistakenly believe that we have to totally agree on all things in order to operate as a system. The contrary is actually true. When we are allowed to be ourselves, explore, understand, and live exactly as we are, we push back a space of safety for those around us. When we ask for support from those around us, we are widening our circle, allowing ourselves and our loved ones to expand, and at the same time inviting safe supports to push back the walls we have imposed around ourselves and each other.

We start here, at this very small circle of safety, to ensure that what we are building fits us and our family. We deserve to stand in the world and not feel squeezed out. The letting-in process can seem very small and lonely as we are doing hard work to set up safe structures. However, as we courageously make the room we need by inviting others into our journey, we open the space around us so we can breathe and we make room for more.

Having done the work of letting others in, we are strengthened for the next step in our process, which is living in the world as our full selves with our full support and love on display. When we know that we belong to these inner circles of safety and we are fortified by their love, it's so much easier to take the step to live our lives as part of an affirming family.

Reflection

Identifying the Inner Rings of Our Personal Circle of Safety

As we continue to build our circles of safety, take time to center yourself and not your loved one. Allow yourself to think of the kinds of support you may need from those closest to you.

* When you think of individuals who can give you non-judgmental support, whom do you think of? Here are some things to consider when building your inner circle.
  * Do you wholeheartedly trust this person/people?
  * Does your loved one trust this person/people?
  * Can you rely on the discretion of this person/people?
  * Do you value their input?
  * Can they separate their experiences from your experiences?
  * Will they allow you to make your own decisions without judgment?
* While it may be ideal to have our circles of safety begin with close friends, if that is not an option for you, try to identify where you might receive nonjudgmental, confidential support in the following areas:
  * Mental Health—Affirming therapists can often be found by googling "LGBTQ+-affirming therapists." You can also narrow choices for therapists

by religious affiliation through sites like Betterhelp. com and Therapytribe.com.

- ○ Religious Support—If you attend an affirming religious community, you can contact your leadership and ask for confidential support. You can also find affirming spiritual directors through Spiritual Directors International's portal online.
- ○ Medical Support—If you find that you are in need of medical support for anxiety, depression, or any other physical or mental issue, finding a doctor who is willing to listen and support you is helpful. Medical doctors as well as holistic practitioners such as chiropractors and acupuncturists have a duty to keep confidentiality and should ethically remain nonjudgmental.

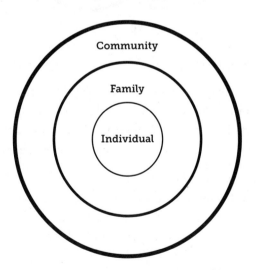

Figure 1: Ring Theory Structure

Exercises

Getting on the Same Page

Combined Circles of Safety

Now that you have taken time separately to think about your circles of safety, share them with each other and see where they overlap.

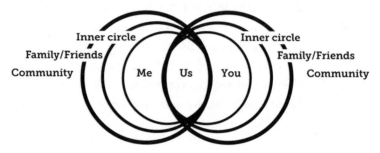

Figure 8: Where Your Circles Meet Mine

Timeline for Safety

If there are individuals or groups in your circles of safety that are in conflict, take some time to talk through the reasons for these hesitations on both sides and the timeline for when it may be possible to find support through these channels.

> Whom would I like to let in?
> Why do I want to let them in?
> What are the roadblocks to letting them in?
> What would need to happen in order for us both to feel safe letting them in?

8

The Family Journey Out

KATIE LEAN-IN: As we sat idling on the runway on our way home from New Mexico on April 1, 2019, I held my breath as Nia pushed *send* on an Instagram message I knew would change our lives forever. Our closest circle of friends and family was aware that Nia was transgender, but this post would let everyone in our sphere of influence know who she really was. I knew Nia would be coming out publicly soon, but I had no idea it would be in an Instagram post on our way home from a weeklong conference. When Nia finally moves into action, things move quickly, and in her need to be known, she crafted a message, asked me to review it, and pressed *post*.

Nia powered down her phone and sat back in her chair, relieved to have let her truth out into the world. I held my breath the entire flight. When we landed in Des Moines, we flipped our phones out of airplane mode, and the dings started pouring in. The cat was out of the bag now, and there was no turning back. The moment we stepped off the plane, we started a new life. She was out, and we turned a page in our family history. We were out as a Queer family. Over the coming months, we would be grappling with what that looked like and fielding questions and opinions from those who didn't quite understand what was going on. We leaned heavily on those we had let in and clung to the freedom we had found in coming out of the shadows and into the light. It was the hardest step we've ever taken as a family and the best decision we could have ever made.

The family journey out will look different for each of us. For some, it may mean an embracing of our own Queer identity, and if that's you, congratulations—we are so happy for you! For others of us, it may mean being welcomed by our current community with open arms with a different vocabulary and lens for our family life. And for others, it may mean leaving old nonaffirming structures and finding or creating a new chosen family and community. Wherever we find ourselves in this journey, there is support available.

When we journey out as a family, we are allowing our new family identity to be seen by all of our community circles. We are trusting in the safety of the structures we have built to hold us up as we live our lives as a family that includes Queer members. For some, this may not feel like a huge shift. For others, especially for those of us who have yet to come out and have only thought of living in a Queer family, our expectations may not match our reality. The truth is that while many people are affirming, accepting, and loving, a vocal, nonaffirming minority still has an influence on our culture. We must remember that gay marriage has only been legal in all fifty US states since 2015 and is under threat to be taken back to the court, and we are still fighting for the rights of gender-expansive and transgender individuals. The world we are walking in as a family with Queer members is not always hospitable to our identities and the identities of those we love.

Setting the Tone

The reason we encourage so much internal work before publicly living as an out family is because the closest family members set the tone for how our loved one is accepted in our circles of influence, including in our extended family, religious groups, and social networks. Especially those of us whose spouse or child is coming out, many of our friends and family are looking to us to gauge reactions. If we come to these conversations with our own sense of confusion or anger, it is likely that those who love us and still have negative or ambivalent attitudes toward Queer identity will follow our lead and reinforce our own struggles. While these friends may think they are supporting us, in the long run, dwelling in the attitudes of others who do not hold the same love and empathy for our loved ones can cause us to pull away and become hardened in our relationship with our Queer family members. The coming-out journey is a difficult one, especially if we encounter friction. When we move through our own internal journey first, we will be more in touch with our own experience and will be better able to understand how we want to move our way through this journey together.

As our loved one comes out, they may request that we, as their trusted family, speak to other family members and members of our social networks about their Queer identity. It is an honor to be asked to do this, and it is deeply needed. Our loved one is likely to have been traversing their journey of sexual or gender identity for the better part of their lives. They have been carrying their identity and wrestling with when, where, and how to come out. The emotional and sometimes physical toll that coming out can have on a person is great. In order to defray some of the burden of constantly explaining themselves to others, especially when they are expecting confrontation, it is not uncommon for those coming out to either ask for or give permission to trusted people in their lives to go ahead and tell others about their Queer identity.

Many people wonder what the best way to tell others about their loved one's Queer identity is. While there is no right way to come out to others on behalf of your loved one, we recommend the following tips:

* Make sure your loved one wants the individual you are telling to know about their identity. Consent is *key*!
* Be factual and brief (i.e., "David recently told me that he is bisexual. It is important to him that you know this is part of who he is").
* Express your support: "I am very proud of him for coming out."
* Answer questions in a straightforward and nonjudgmental manner: "Bisexuality is when someone is attracted to both men and women. Yes, David may date and eventually marry a woman, but that doesn't mean he is no longer bisexual."
* If you are unsure how to answer a question, be honest: "I can't speak to that particular question, but I have found PFLAG to be a wonderful resource."

* Set boundaries: "I know you may not agree with David or our choice to support him, but we are not changing our minds, and it is not up for discussion."
* Invite positive interaction: "I am sure that David would appreciate your support. If you want to send him a text expressing your love and support, that would be great."

When we are in touch with our own dedication to our loved one, it is far easier to talk with others, both supportive and not. It is incredibly important that when we speak to others about our loved one's Queer identity, we are honest about our own process and also firm in our support. It is okay to say we have struggled or that we were shocked as long as we are able to follow up these statements with loving affirmation for our Queer family members.

For those of us who are still struggling with affirmation of our loved one's identity, we encourage deep self-reflection and a continuation of the journey to acceptance. If this is where you find yourself, let someone else who has reached the place of acceptance lead the way in telling others about your loved one's identity. All of us desire and deserve acceptance, but the truth is we don't have to fully accept our loved one's gender or sexual identity to still treat them with love and respect and present who they are to others in a way that honors them. As you work toward acceptance, we suggest focusing on the respect you have for the process your loved one is going through and work toward honoring them with your words. We don't have to be immediately thrilled with our loved one's journey, but we can respect their courage and vulnerability. It's okay to still be in process ourselves as long as we do not project our own struggles onto our loved one or those around us. We can still remain factual and direct attention toward the areas of respect that we can honor at this time.

When we are invited into the process of our loved one's coming out, we have been gifted a responsibility. Our loved one has given us their trust, and our response should be to carry their truth with dignity and honor. The process of coming out to family or community members can sometimes feel daunting and draining, especially when the process is slow, individual, and met with some resistance. Even when we don't encounter resistance, the responsibility of disclosing our loved one's identity can become tiring and seem all-consuming. This is not the case for everyone, but for those family members who experience coming out this way, it is important to remember that we are acting in solidarity with our loved one and giving them the gift of loving them through our actions. Helping them come out, especially when the circumstances are difficult, is an act of radical love that binds us together.

Talking the Talk

Once the major work of coming out is done, we are left living our lives in a new dynamic. We say *major work* because throughout your family life, there will be times when disclosure becomes a choice. For transgender family members, the initial coming out will be a seismic shift. However, as they transition, they may be able to decide whom they would like to disclose their gender identity to. This will need to be a family discussion as you meet new people and enter new systems, especially those systems with rigid gender roles. Disclosure may be optional for some trans and gender-expansive individuals, and being on the same page about that as a family is key.

Disclosure of sexual identity may look different for different families. Nonpartnered family members with Queer sexual identities may or may not choose to divulge that information to everyone. Some partnered Queer folks may also have discernment around whom they tell and when. It is vitally important that the expectations around the disclosure of a family member's identity are clear to all members of the family.

For us, our family identity changed rapidly. Not only did Nia transition, but because of her transition, Katie was also "outed" as Queer. However, the time it took for others and Katie herself to recognize her Queer identity lagged behind Nia's transition. So much focus was rightfully placed on Nia's journey. It took time for Katie to process her own identity and then come out herself. Those around us also had to see Nia as a woman before they could recognize Katie's Queer identity, all of which took time. Our ability to hold deeply ingrained structures in our brains is astonishing. In fact, it would not surprise us if someone who knows us reads this book and realizes for the first time that Katie is indeed Queer. Our story exemplifies how difficult it can be to reroute the way we think about ourselves and the ways others see us.

This is why it is important to put words to our new family dynamic. We have to start addressing our family life in the way that suits *our* family. If our family member comes out as trans-nonbinary, it is important we immediately begin using their pronouns, name, and any other defining terms they have asked us to use. When our family member comes out as lesbian, we stop asking questions about their boyfriends or guy crushes. We stop saying, "the man you will marry," and we start using the word *girlfriend* or *wife*. For any number of gender and sexual identities, there are shifts to be made in our language. By making these shifts, we begin telling our brain to align with our family member's identity. We need to say the words in our head, out loud, to ourselves, and to others. We need to change our contact list on our phones to reflect our trans loved one's name. We need to say that our son's "good friend" is indeed his boyfriend. By changing our language, we solidify in our bodies what we know to be true, and it becomes natural over time. The more we resist a change in our language, the more difficult it will become to accept the shifts that are happening in regard to our loved one's identity and our relationship to them.

We suggest practicing when you have the chance and not just when you are in the presence of your loved one. When you sit down to talk with others who know your loved one's identity, use their correct identifiers. Say their name out loud until you can say it without hesitation. Practice saying the words that make you uncomfortable or sound foreign because they haven't been a part of your vernacular until you are comfortable and it sounds natural. We are building muscle memory around our loved one's identity and the way we interact with them. Language is an important part of building a strong family unit in which everyone feels safe and loved.

Living as a Conspicuous Family

The building blocks of owning our feelings around our loved one's identity and solidifying our affirmation of them through our thoughts and speech will be vital in living as a happy and healthy family with an out family member. The truth is, when we begin to walk into the world with our new family identity, it feels different. Not for everyone, and not at all times, but there will be moments and places where our families will be conspicuous. We will draw attention, both good and bad, depending on where we are, and having firm modes of affirmation within ourselves will be essential to live as a proud unit.

When Nia came out, we were already living life as a conspicuous family because of our son who has a disability and also adopted. Everywhere we went, we drew attention. There was no disguising that we were an interracial adoptive family or that our four-year-old used a walker to get around. Everywhere we went, there seemed to be a flashing light over our heads that said "look over here!" The stares, sideways glances, uninvited help, and unsolicited prayers for healing happened every time we left our house. It was exhausting, to say the least. To be fair, most people are not malicious or cruel. They are simply curious about something that is out of their ordinary. However, even well-meaning interactions left us exhausted after something as simple as a family outing to the park.

Part of Nia's coming out involved coming to grips with being a conspicuous family. We were already living a life where people saw and judged us on a daily basis. We couldn't hide from it, and when we finally accepted the reality that our lives would include some level of visibility, we realized that we could adjust to it as our new normal. We'd already blown *typical* out of the water, and that released us from the expectation that we should fit into an identity that was restrictive to us. We find this freedom to be one of the great gifts of Queer identity, and once you find that freedom, there really is no returning to old ways of contorting ourselves to fit into something that just isn't made for us.

Conspicuous life will be a reality for most Queer individuals and families at some point, and we find that the spotlight is brighter in some places than in others. In our religious space, the spotlight after Nia came out was blazing to the point of discomfort and pain for us. In both good and difficult ways, we were very visible in the midwestern city that we grew up in. However, after moving to the East Coast, we have found that we are far less conspicuous as people here seem to have more awareness of trans identity, Queer coupling, and varying physical abilities. Our new home city has a familiarity with diversity that was not as developed where we had been. Each family has to assess the intensity of the spotlight they live in and what they can live with. It's okay to feel uncomfortable with a new level of visibility. In healthy environments combined with our own personal work, this intensity will cool over time.

While not every family will be Queer-forward all the time, there will be times in all of our lives when Queer identity will set us apart. Folks will ask questions. There will be times when you have to clarify your loved one's identity. You will hear others disagree with your family structure, and you may find yourself defending your loved one and yourself. We don't point out this reality to scare you. In fact, the opposite. If we are aware of how conspicuous our families may be, we will be ready for it. We can prepare for the fact that other parents may have concerns over our daughter taking her girlfriend to the prom. We can write scripts for when our spouse is misgendered in public. We can dig deep into our reservoirs of love and find pride in ourselves and our families. We can understand that our family is a gift and that our willingness to show up and be seen in the world is a harbinger of hope for so many others that need to know that their Queer identity is beautiful and they are worthy of the love and support of a family.

Discovering Family Identity

Through our journey with our family members, we may begin to see new parts of ourselves. The night that Nia let Katie in on her gender journey, Katie saw a woman at a restaurant with a haircut that she loved and thought to herself, *If Nia can do this, I can certainly get the haircut I want.* The next week, Katie buzzed a triangular undercut into her long, thick hair and within a few months had chopped it into a short pixie, a style she'd always wanted but avoided because of the unspoken cultural importance of long hair in our religious context. This was the beginning of Katie's eyes being opened to the ways in which she'd molded herself to the expectations of others instead of following her true desires for herself.

A hairstyle may seem like a silly thing to avoid because of cultural expectation, but the number of women Katie meets who express how much they wish they could cut their hair is remarkable. It's not always about sexual or gender identity or a push against a religious identifier. Sometimes it's as simple as not wanting to break some unwritten beauty standard for round faces or mature women. Katie has now kept a short, brightly colored pixie for over five years and still receives remarks about how much other people wish they were brave enough to take that risk. It's a simple thing worth noting because it tells us how often we bend a knee to external expectations, either implicit or explicit. So many of us deprive ourselves of the experience of simple joys because we have internalized a set of rules never meant for us.

Hair was just the beginning for Katie in discovering her own identity. It was a marker that helped guide her toward a truer version of herself until she could finally embrace her own Queer identity. Katie likes to say that Nia gifted her the awareness of her own Queerness. By choosing bravery over the fear of the unknown and choosing to be true to herself, Nia allowed Katie to break free from the rigid standards she had been holding herself to. It seemed like there were rules for engagement everywhere, but Nia was taking a step outside of those rules and asking if they were even necessary. Her ability to ask difficult questions allowed room for answers. Those answers included Katie's Queer identity. Nia never asked Katie to be Queer; she simply gave Katie the ability to see herself.

In our experience, this is not uncommon in families and close friend groups after a member comes out. It takes a huge amount of courage to own your identity, and when someone else goes before us and shows us a part of ourselves, it can make it easier for us to come out. Some of us who walk the coming-out journey with our loved ones will be gifted the opportunity to see ourselves, some for the first time. We can then lean on our loved one as we traverse our own personal journey of coming out. This is a beautiful representation of mutuality in relationship that leads to healing.

KATIE LEAN-IN FOR SPOUSES: For those of us who are walking the coming-out journey with a spouse or partner, their gender and sexual identity will have a direct impact on us. We will have to undertake an intense amount of personal work to understand our own emotions connected to their journey. When Nia came out to me, I was living in the assumption that I was straight. I never had to think about my sexual identity. Nia was the first person I had ever loved, ever kissed, ever had sex with, so all I knew is that I loved Nia and was attracted to her. Our friends joked that my sexual identity was Nia-sexual. While this was a great placeholder for me until I understood myself a little better; it wasn't a label that was ultimately fair to me or to Nia. I had to do the internal work to understand my own attractions and desires.

I discovered that I had a lot of capacity inside of my sexual identity. So much so that I am not ready to narrow myself beyond the label of Queer. My personality lends itself to familiarity and comfort inside of unknowing, but that doesn't mean I still didn't wrestle with who I am inside of our marriage and sexual partnership. Nia's transition also meant transition for me, and I wanted to be true to myself just as much as I wanted to be true to her.

As we go through this journey with our partner, we have to be able to widen our view beyond this particular relationship and understand our sexual needs for ourselves. Understanding our own attractions is an important facet of human life, and our sexuality should not be something we sacrifice for the identity of another person. If we trade our own sexual or gender identity for our partner's, we are simply swapping who is repressing themselves. Good partnerships should lead to more expansive self-identification, even if that means the way we engage in that partnership needs to end.

For those whose partner comes out as an incompatible orientation, such as a husband coming out as gay and a wife who is straight, the work is not who will give up their sexual identity for the other but rather how we stay true to ourselves while loving each other well. This may mean that the dynamic of our relationship changes from married sexual partners to friends and confidants. When Nia came out, I worried because I knew I wasn't a lesbian, but I wasn't sure I was strictly straight. I asked my therapist for advice, and she led me through a thought experiment so I could understand myself a little better. She offered a myriad of possibilities, one being that I might not be as straight as I thought and others such as polyamory—an opening of our marriage to more than one partner—or platonic partnership outside of a marriage relationship. While the exercise didn't give me concrete answers as to what my sexual identity is, it did help me narrow down what I didn't want. The rest I left up to understanding as I lived it.

As partners, the way our relationships look may have to change based on our sexual and gender identities. In order to make room for all of who we are, we may need to expand on our ideas of what a traditional family looks like and how partners and friends operate. This will be a painful process, but when we are true to ourselves, we are able to live a freer, more satisfying life. We show those around us that just because things don't work out how we thought they should, it doesn't mean that things are bad. We are adjustable creatures. If we are willing to own ourselves and not blame one another for our growth and discovery, we can participate in a world of creative love. We can lead the way. It starts with us.

Becoming an Accomplice

Of course, not all family members will find a Queer identity within themselves. However, we hope family members will find their identity as, what Darnell L. Moore, author of *No Ashes in the Fire*, calls an *accomplice*.[1] While allyship is good and necessary, an accomplice walks closely with those whose identities are perceived as different in some way. An accomplice is the definition of someone who is with us, not just for us.

Good allies advocate for friends and stand up for others when they are hurting. They are a vital part of communal change. However, allyship can skew performative when we lack deep relational understanding and interdependence. Allies send money, attend protests, use their voices through voting, and shut down homophobic and transphobic conversations. Accomplices are those who are living Queer reality right now, not necessarily in their bodies but in their relationships with Queer folks.

Accomplices come in many forms. They are parents who advocate for their child's gender-affirming care. They are siblings who host Thanksgiving dinner when their parents won't acknowledge their brother's boyfriend. They are spouses who encourage their partner to explore their gender identity and press for constructive solutions for both their identity and their partner's. Accomplices fend off attacks, sometimes by taking the brunt of them. They sit with us when no one else will, and they become our family when ours refuses to acknowledge our identity.

Our five most treasured accomplices are our children. Early in her transition process, Nia expressed worry to her therapist about our kids. She was worried that her coming out would throw their world into chaos. Her therapist suggested that by living her true self with our kids, they would be able to see who she was fully and be unafraid to live their own authentic lives. On top of that, she suggested that our kids would reflexively defend her and let their love lead the way. I mean, you try telling a six-year-old that their love for their parents is wrong. We also quickly realized that if someone is willing to fight your kid on why they should not love you for who you are, it's pretty obvious if they should be in your life or not. Newsflash: they should not. Allowing our kids to own their feelings about Nia's transition and speak their love for their mothers out loud has been sustaining for the both of us and healing for those around us who thought being Queer meant being a subpar parent.

About a year after coming out publicly, our kids' school in rural Iowa had a Mother's Day writing contest. Two of our children decided to write about Nia. Our kids had been at this school before Nia's transition, and the school knew what our kids had gone through in order for Nia to live as herself. As a faculty, they judged the contributions from each grade and gave out awards of floral certificates to the students they felt expressed their love for their mom in the most eloquent ways. Our two kids who wrote about Nia each won their grade level and came home beaming with pride. They were forthright in their essays about Nia's transition and their love for her as their mother. It was a beautiful representation of the love of a child for a parent and how it touches the hearts of others. Their writing about Nia and the validation of our story by the school healed something deep inside both of us and gave us strength to keep going when the path was difficult.

When we are willing to live our lives alongside our loved one, acknowledging their journey as a Queer individual and taking an active part in that life, we are accomplices. We are family. We trust our loved one's experiences, and we believe them when they tell us who they are and what they are going through because, oftentimes, as good accomplices, we are there to see it firsthand. Just as our four biological children don't have to be adopted to be a part of an adoptive family, we don't have to be Queer to be a part of a Queer family. Our family becomes Queer when we allow ourselves to be fundamentally changed and we live inside of this system with genuine love. We don't necessarily assume a Queer identity, but we choose a Queer family system. We will walk in this world differently knowing what it takes to love through hardship and support through pain.

The journey out is complex, nonlinear, and full of surprises both great and small. There is no one prescription for how stepping out into the world as a Queer family should go and no one outcome for all people. Embracing the *why* of our family coming-out process is infinitely more important than the *what* of our actions. Remember: there is no perfect way to live in this world or navigate the journey of coming out and living out as a family. In fact, the process is so full of wins, losses, pains, and joys that we have to reach beyond the categorizations of good and bad and embrace the Queer energy of life. We get to live in a much richer reality that life doesn't always have defined answers, but we instead are invited to be creators of love in the world. We make space for more by being ourselves and living our lives exactly as we are.

Exercise

Practice Difficult Conversations

If you anticipate difficulty with family members or friends on coming out yourself or on behalf of your loved one, first ask yourself a few clarifying questions:

* Is this person genuinely interested in the well-being of my family?
* Do I want this person in my life?
* Is this person someone who can hear what I have to say?

✳ Can I safely, both physically and emotionally, have a conversation with this person?

If you are committed to retaining a relationship with this person, take time to practice with an accomplice what you want to say and how you want to say it. Think of several scenarios and have your partner push back on you as a way to practice what you want to say in case the conversation goes to a difficult place, and if you anticipate that, bring your accomplice along for the conversation. Don't forget to practice positive responses as well. People will surprise you in every way in this process. Don't pigeonhole people into singular responses. We want to be prepared, not project our fears onto others.

9

An Invitation to Community

When you come to visit our home, the first thing you will notice after we welcome you at the front door is our stairwell filled with photos from our vow renewal. The first faces we see as we descend into our days and the last faces we see when we go up to bed at night are those of our dearest friends and family. These photos serve as a reminder of our community that walked beside us during our coming-out journey and has supported us as we've launched into the world as ourselves.

During our ceremony, we stood in a circle with these accomplices and shared a moment of knowing that only those who have walked through the fire together can truly understand. We had each, in turn, supported one another through difficult life circumstances and celebrated together when we triumphed. These beautiful individuals had shared their lives with us in both the good times and the bad. They had held us as we cried, celebrated with us as we found ourselves, and shared with us as we moved through our family's greatest transition. Even after we moved across the country from Iowa to Maryland, we continue to carry this community in our hearts. The bond we created has transcended our physical space and sustains our spirits in our new home.

Recently, we have watched as members of this community have continued the fight for equality for transgender individuals in our home state of Iowa. As we write this book, new bills have been passed to ban life-saving gender-affirming care for minors, and a whole slew of bills are being proposed to strip away the rights of our Queer siblings. We mourn for what is happening in a state we have loved and around the country. And we are grateful for a community of people who are willing to stand up for what is right and love those who are being mistreated by our government. It is the community, made up of loving individuals, that will sustain Queer families and change the tide of public opinion.

It should come as no surprise that Queer individuals and families are encountering opposition, both personally and within the greater societal context. All you have to do is turn on the news lately, and you'll see another politician or celebrity news personality putting the "issues" of gay marriage, transgender identity, and discussions of LGBTQ+ identities in schools on blast. Who we are as individuals has been weaponized in a culture war with an enormous gulf between rhetoric and lived experience.

When Nia came out, we saw this happening firsthand in our home state of Iowa. In fact, Nia's first public outing as herself was to attend a rally at our state capitol protesting anti-trans laws that were being put forth by the president and others in political power. The rhetoric around trans bodies continued, and still continues, to accelerate to a point that when Nia came out publicly, one of the first things we decided we needed to do was to reach out to the authors of some of these harmful bills in our state and ask for a meeting. Three of these lawmakers took us up on this offer.

We sat knee to knee with these three humans in the halls of our state capitol and showed them what it meant to be a Queer family. We explained our lives, our children, our faith, and our struggles. Their lack of knowledge on transgender issues was obvious. From the process of getting on hormones to trans men using women's bathrooms, the issues we had to explain to them were numerous. To their credit, they asked questions and listened intently. However, it was clear that as much as we could show them who we are, the fact is that for some of them, anti-LGBTQ+ rhetoric is what put them in office, and it was sustaining their careers. These were the people making decisions for us. These were the people making decisions for our children. It's difficult to realize that the state you have grown up in and loved is actively pushing you out to satisfy baseless concerns with little factual information and even less scientifically backed evidence. Our experience and conversation with these legislators unfortunately did not do much to stem the onslaught of anti-LGBTQ+ bills introduced by the state government; however, sharing our experience with them meant that at least on the next batch of bills that were similar, the folks we had met with didn't sponsor them.

This is why community is so important. True community that ebbs and flows, that listens to its members and fluidly responds with trustworthy interdependence, is what ultimately can heal our divided hearts. This kind of community reaches beyond the idea that only my story matters by acknowledging that all stories matter because all stories intersect. There is an overlap between my story and your story. When we can come together, acknowledging that we each hold a very specific and precious piece of the whole story, we realize that we need each other in order to live lives of love and freedom. The journey may be uncomfortable, but that doesn't mean it is not worth it.

Entering the Unknown

In order to become a transformative community, we have to put aside the notion that we know all things. We have to embrace the unknown. This is perhaps one of the most difficult steps in becoming a community of change. Most of us are under the erroneous impression that in order to effect change and make a difference, we have to know everything. This is such an insidious lie perpetuated by powerful people who have access to unlimited education and modes of communication. By believing that we must know everything before we can make a step in the right direction, we prevent ourselves from loving well in the midst of change.

In the current climate in the United States, we have placed so much emphasis on "knowing the issues" that we have forgotten to know each other. Statistics are biased. News stories are inflated. Politicians don't have to tell us the truth. Yet we are listening more to social media influencers than we are to the lived experience of our neighbors and friends. We take too much comfort in what is reported to us and far too little risk in asking ourselves and each other the true story of who we are.

When we begin opening up to each other, we realize that hope for our future doesn't belong to politicians and billionaires. It belongs to strong communities made up of individuals who own their stories, listen intently to the experiences of others, and find the common ground of love. As writer and social activist Alice Walker said, "We are the ones we've been waiting for."[1]

Friends, we need each other so desperately. As much as our Queer siblings need community, our communities need our Queer siblings. We can hold each other up. Our dear friend Kristin gifted us a beautiful illustration of the importance of leaning on one another. She reminded us that when contractors find weak spots in a home, they look at the joists and see which ones need shoring up. In order to reinforce sagging, splintered, or weak joists, they will often sandwich the weak joist with new beams in a process called *sistering*. This is what it means to live inside of a community that holds one another up. When I am weak, you sister me. When you are weak, I sister you. We come alongside each other, and in doing so, we make each other stronger than we have ever been. It's not only that the strong beams fortify the weaker but the delicate beam also allows the solid beams to become part of the structure. Without the older beam, the new beams have nothing to hold on to.

In the same way, we fortify each other. At any given time in our lives, we will experience being both the broken beam and the remedy. We will be called into community by those who need our strength, and we will cling to them as our community ages and withstands the winds of change. Those who have already faced the wilderness of uncertainty will be able to remind us that love is stronger than hate, and as a community, we can weather the storm together.

KRISTIN LEAN-IN: Glennon Doyle shares the idea of sistering, and it is one that has made a profound impact on how I live my life.[2] Relying on each other is such a sacred act of mutual trust. It's when we can help each other feel seen, and held, and cared for. We are not meant to carry loads alone, despite what some want us to believe. Because when we are broken, we are quiet. We don't have the strength to resist, or rise up, or invoke change. But when we are held up by others who are standing next to us, things begin to shift. When Nia let me in by sharing her true self, it was the beginning of a sistering in the truest sense. It meant being vulnerable because while the decision to sister is never difficult, the act itself can be. It's saying, "I don't have the answers, but we will learn together." Some days, it means quiet hikes together, and some days it means attending a political rally with hundreds of others. It's dismantling previous beliefs and hard, beautiful conversations. It's "just checking-in" phone calls and worry that keeps you up late at night. Sistering is joy, and laughter, and pain, and heartache. Sistering is holding on to each other because we are not meant to carry things alone.

Loving without Judgment or Fear

Very early in our journey toward greater freedom, we decided to get our first tattoos together. At the time, Katie was helping our pastor to prepare a series of sermons based on the book of 1 John in the New Testament. 1 John 4:18 says, "There is no fear in love. But perfect love drives out fear, because fear has to do with punishment. The one who fears is not made perfect in love."[3] As we were coming home from church one day, Nia turned to Katie and said, "I know what our first tattoo should be." Katie looked at Nia and said, "Is it 'perfect love'?" Nia just laughed, and a few weeks later, we both had the words *perfect love* tattooed onto our wrists, Katie's in Nia's handwriting, Nia's in its original Greek, τέλέια αγάπη.

The Greek translation for the word *perfect* in 1 John 4:18 is τέλειος (*telios*), which means "having reached its end" or "complete."[4] We had spent our lives being afraid of a God who would punish us if we didn't get everything right. We were taught that hell is real, unrelenting torment and that we should accept Jesus as our savior so that he could hold back God's wrath so we didn't get what we deserved, which was an eternity in hell.

This kind of theological manipulation caused us a great deal of pain in our childhoods. We know many people who grew up similarly who have battled with anxiety and depression trying to reconcile a God who says they love us in one breath but would condemn us to hell for lying to our parents, hitting our brother, or being gay in the next. However, this verse in 1 John was the beam of light we had been waiting for. Complete, perfectly complete, love required no fear because punishment was not the price that God requires for God's love. People invented this kind of punishment. We were able to lose the chains of perfection in our actions and seek a more complete love.

When Nia came out, this kind of complete love was the guiding principle in the way Katie chose to move forward. It was an easy way to cut through the bullshit concerning the issues of Nia's transgender identity and see her. Choosing to love Nia despite what Katie thought she knew was the best decision she had ever made. Can we say there has been no fear? Absolutely not. Choosing to love in the face of hate and bigotry and a life-time of learning that who you are will send you to hell is incredibly difficult and wildly scary. However, by choosing to love, we know that we can push through that fear because punishment isn't waiting for us—more love is.

The only way we can know this now is because we chose to let go of what we thought we knew then. Those who still make up our community did the same thing. They let go of what they thought they knew about Nia and Katie and sexuality and gender and let their new ideas be shaped by their experience of us and their love for us. They let go of fear, recognizing that waiting for punishment and trying to work inside a notion of perfection do nothing but divide us. Looking for love and working toward that goal unite us. It makes us whole. It completes us.

We live in a world that is thirsty to cast judgment. You don't have to have grown up in a religious context to know that the threat of some kind of punishment is a tool that has been used for centuries to keep people in line and deflect responsibility for even greater harms. It's much easier to blame the unruly masses than to look inside of our own communal ways of being, our pull toward power, and our individual prejudices and take stock of what needs to change for the greater good. However, when we stop focusing on blame and start accepting that we have agency to love, we realize that love can be a force for change.

Imagine communities of people creating space for love beyond fear. Honoring one another's experiences and calling those they disagree with into conversation instead of calling them out. Not everyone will choose to enter this kind of community. Some will insist on keeping the powerful status quo. That's up to them. However, we can still choose the power of love, to see others as human beings who are struggling and getting it wrong. We can still call out evils as we see them, and we can do it in love. We can resist oppression and hatred through love. When we choose to love, we choose something that is bigger than ourselves. As Dr. Martin Luther King Jr. expressed in a handwritten note, "Love is the greatest force in the universe. It is the heartbeat of the moral cosmos. He who loves is a participant in the being of God."[5]

Humanity is a race in process. We are continually learning, growing, and evolving. These steps toward our higher selves will come with intense moments of backlash and resistance, but that doesn't mean that our progress toward a greater love isn't worth it. In fact, love is the only thing worth moving toward. If not, where are we going? What are we doing? If we can't learn to love well through all of our faults and failings, we will be left with very little of what it is that makes us human. None of us are perfect, but if we are willing to make space for one another, we can progress.

Breaking the Binary

One way we continue that progression is to stop living so rigidly inside of the arbitrary lines that we have drawn that separate us from each other. One of the great gifts of Queer identity is that it blurs the lines of expectation and allows us to see things in a different way. As a friend of Katie's once expressed, Queer identity allows us to pull back the bars on the cages we have made for ourselves. We are so used to living in these boxes that we don't realize it until someone comes along and shakes us awake.

NIA LEAN-IN: I remember the first time that I realized how symbiotic the coming-out process within a community could be. I had recently come out to a small group of friends whom Katie and I and our family regularly had dinner with. While our friends weren't certain what my gender transition would mean for our family, they were all very supportive and inquired thoughtfully after I had invited any questions they might have. One friend in particular asked me what I thought I might lose or how my parenting might change if I identified as a mom to my kids instead of a dad. At first thought, there were of course a lot of things that I thought might change based on the societal gender roles that I had grown up with my whole life and even inside of my own marriage. But this question caused me to take a moment of deep reflection on what it actually would mean for me to identify as a mom to my kids instead of a dad. I could still teach my boys how to shave and could talk to them about sexuality and love interests and things they might experience as a young man, as I had had those same experiences. I could take all my kids fishing or play catch with them, things that "typical dads" do with their children. After a long reflection, I realized that everything that I had assigned a gender label to, like being a stern father or a nurturing mother, was simply just moving through the world in different ways. These ways of being and ways of interacting with our children, although associated with gender, actually had nothing to do with gender. Yes, more fathers may be interested in fishing and therefore be more apt to take their kids fishing, but mothers do this too. Stepping back further outside of my own experience, I thought about single parents who are everything to their children. Soon the boxes I had created around gender expectations were breaking down. The question from my friend served to blow the box that I had built for myself to smithereens. My response to her question, which was my perception that not much, if anything, would have to change when I identify as a mom instead of a dad to my kids, in turn has changed the perception of my community many times over. I've used this example on countless occasions, and people have told me that it has been meaningful for them to examine their own bias and understanding of gender roles and expectations in their own lives. One simple question inside of a community committed to growth and healing can truly change the way we live life together.

The divisions in our culture are real and ubiquitous. We are divided by our race, our gender, our religion, and our politics. There is very little room for gray in our culture at the current moment. There is a good reason for this. Many underrepresented groups, including Queer individuals, have the ability and feel the responsibility to use our voices and leverage what power we do have to create equity for those who have historically been silenced. With the rise of social media, we have more exposure than ever, and as the world becomes increasingly more accepting, many of us choose to be more visible. This will inevitably lead to a backlash from those who feel they are losing something simply because Queer people have the same freedoms and rights as they do. Because of the way that power dynamics work, the thought of sharing often feels like someone is stealing from us when, in reality, all we want is to belong.

As a result, all of us feel as though we have to dig our heels in. What we can learn from Queer identity is that there is always a third, or fourth, or twelfth way. We can learn to Queer the systems that we live in. Queering our systems simply means to challenge them in a new way, especially in the areas of gender and sexuality. When we Queer the binary of who is right and who is wrong, we can assess to see if there is a more nuanced and beautiful way to engage with one another.

One of our favorite representations of this idea is the writer and activist ALOK. ALOK is a nonbinary, genderqueer poet who is incredibly vivacious and forward in their Queer representation and also lovingly invitational to those who disagree. In their work, ALOK writes and performs about the reality of living between and beyond binaries and how scary that can be for those in our communities who have been hurt by hyper masculinization and feminization. ALOK calls out our overidentification with these labels and invites listeners to reach beyond who we have been told to be to find who we truly are. In their beautiful poem *Your Wound, My Garden,* they invite us to see them, and all genderqueer people, at the intersection of our collective wounding and thriving by boldly proclaiming,

> *your wound is my garden,*
> *i have found life here in the places you have left for dead.*
> *watch me bloom.*[6]

ALOK stands like a beacon of hope for those who desperately need to heal from the divides within themselves. ALOK reminds us that creativity, beauty, and self-expression are the answers to the ways in which we've been conditioned to hate through cultural norms. Their consistent call to heal from wounding resounds in their beautiful work as they call us to ponder the idea "what if love, then, is the organizing force of the universe?"[7]

This is what Queer identity does. It draws us into conversation about what it means to be ourselves in our bodies and conversation about the ways that we love. This is also why Queer identity can feel threatening to communal structures that are built on binary ideas about gender and sexual identity. So many of us carry wounds surrounding these identifiers, and all of us have been handed scripts about what is and isn't appropriate for us depending on our gender and our roles in a sexual relationship.

Growing up, Katie was told that her curiosity, vivacity, and desire to preach were too masculine. She was routinely told that her talents were only appropriate for teaching women and children. She was prayed over to be submissive and told to be quiet and stay in line. The explicit and implicit expectations of our complementarian religious environment wounded Katie's sense of her own femininity. When Nia came out, and Katie had to face the abuse she had endured throughout her life, she realized the religious community around us was not safe for her. It was a devastating blow, and Katie could have easily blamed Nia for not conforming to the expectations of the community as she had. However, instead of asking Nia to keep contorting herself into a place where she didn't fit, she accepted Nia's invitation to step out into a more spacious place where we could both be ourselves. Nia provided a means for Katie to understand just how deeply she had been harmed and also provided her with a way out. Together we would build the community we needed. Starting with our family.

Creating Sanctuaries of Peace

Philosopher, author, and poet Dr. Bayo Akomolafe[8] calls this kind of community-building *making sanctuary at the rupture.* In his work as a climate activist and racial justice advocate, Dr. Akomolafe invites us to imagine what it would be like to create sanctuaries at the places we are most wounded. As ALOK alludes to in *Your Wounds, My Garden*, Queer identity grows in the rifts between the binary. In the places where we have had to divide ourselves to fit inside of the status quo of gender and sexual identity, Queer folks create shelter for healing simply by existing.

What would it look like for us to live in the sanctuary of that shelter instead of going to war against it? What would sheltering together look like as opposed to animosity? We are so far removed from peace that it's hard to actually understand what it would look and feel like. Our bodies have been rewired, in some ways, to expect the next emotional, psychological, and even physical blow. Recently, our world has dealt with war, pandemic, natural disasters, rapid climate change, attacks on personal freedoms, ongoing racism, and deeply divisive political rhetoric. Our nervous systems have been activated for years to protect against the next crushing blow. We need peace, but it feels dangerous to allow ourselves to let down long enough to sink into a balanced state of homeostasis.

It is up to us to grow these gardens of safety and peace. We can encourage places of beauty that remind us what it is to be human. We can construct sanctuaries where we need them the most. When we are open to tilling the soil around our deep wounds of gender and sexuality, we can begin to sow seeds of good and healthy human interaction. We can grow gardens full of hydrangeas and roses, daisies and pansies. We can embrace the diversity it takes to make something truly beautiful. Katie's mom is an incredible gardener, and watching her carefully choose where each flower, plant, bird bath, and statue belongs is a lesson in caretaking beauty. She's never planted a whole garden full of one type of plant. Each garden has always been a beautiful symphony of colors, textures, shapes, and sizes. Her creations invite her grandchildren to come and play and guests to her home to sit and stay. She knows the feeling she wants, and she cultivates it carefully.

This is what community can be. Our communities can be places where all people are tenderly cared for and loved into the beauty they innately possess. They can be places where we want to sit and linger because we know we are seen and loved exactly as we are. They can be places not of right and wrong but of being. We can build sanctuaries where people can find shelter from the storm and be renewed and refreshed. We can do all of these things, but we cannot do them apart from one another. It takes each of us, tilling and growing, watering and thriving. We have to stop treating our communities like boardrooms with tables too small for everyone and start seeing them as expanding gardens of beauty and peace. In order to do this, we have to be willing to listen, trust, and participate together. In order for our world to heal, we have to start at the places we hurt.

Exercise for Community Members

Questions for exploring gender and sexual harm for community members

* Can you remember a time in your life when you were shamed for acting counter to the expectation for your

gender? How did that make you feel? Did you change in any way?

* What expectations have been placed on you because of your gender? How do you feel about these expectations?

* What roles have you taken on because of your gender? Would you have taken on that role without the expectation?

* How have sexual norms affected how you feel about your:

  o body image and looks in general?
  o aging process?
  o gender identification?
  o self-esteem?
  o emotional disposition (i.e., introversion or extroversion)?

* If there were no gender or sexual expectations on you, how would you choose to move through the world?

10

Embracing Queer Community

When our children were young, they loved nature shows like the *Wild Kratts* and the *Octonauts*, which taught our kiddos all about animals and sea life. These programs geared their content toward little minds and made learning about zoology fun. One concept that captured our attention was that of mutuality, the idea that two organisms from different species rely on one another for support. One such example of this kind of relationship is the black rhinoceros and the red-billed oxpecker. You may have seen pictures of this tiny bird perched on the haunches of a giant horned rhino. It's such a cute combination that also has incredible utility.

Red-billed oxpeckers perch themselves on the bodies of black rhinos to gather food in the form of parasites and ticks. As they work their way around the body of the rhino, they receive sustenance from their thick-skinned friend, and the rhino gets cleaned and has dangerous parasites and disease-carrying ticks removed from its hide. The relationship between this gigantic mammal and this tiny bird helps both of them to thrive. One without the other begins to suffer. The relationship, of course, is not without its hang-ups, such as pesky beaks digging into open wounds and swats from a coarse bristled tail. However, the benefits that each receives from the relationship make the trials of cohabitating worth it for both members of the relationship.

A deeper kind of mutuality also exists in the natural world, which is called *symbiosis*. This relationship evolves over time, making reliance on another species vital to the life of one or both members of the relationship. Over the course of time, the species become so reliant on one another that they are inseparable, as is the case for the fig wasp and the fig. The relationship between these two species not only perpetuates the two species but also feeds entire ecosystems.

Figs are unique as they do not have blooms that are exposed, but rather their flowers are inverted and require a very specific kind of pollinator. The fig wasp has evolved over time to be able to wriggle her way into the heart of the fig carrying nourishing pollen and her fertilized eggs. However, her journey to the heart of the fig requires the loss of her wings as the access point to the fig is very tight.

Once inside the fig, the wasp spreads the pollen she has gathered from the fig in which she was born, lays her eggs, and then dies. The fig will compost her body into nourishment as it grows. When the wasp's eggs hatch, the males mate with the females, and the females gather pollen from the now-mature flowers inside of the fig. The male fig wasps wriggle out, losing their wings and sacrificing their lives to allow the females enough space to safely emerge from inside in order to find their way to the next fig to pollinate. The fig provides the safe space for the wasp to procreate, while the wasp provides the fig with the nourishment it requires to grow.

Figs are the underpinning of many ecosystems, feeding animals and birds, creating shade, and protecting soil. Researchers have found that when the ratio of figs and wasps is askew, whole ecosystems are put at risk. Each member of the relationship is essential for the health and vitality of the whole.[1]

As humans, who too often see ourselves as somehow apart from nature, we marvel at these ideas of mutuality and symbiosis but think ourselves beyond the need for such relationships. This simply isn't true. However, the difficulty and sometimes outright risk of these relationships often cause us to become overwhelmed by fear that turns to anger. Instead of taking the hand of the one who can help to heal us, we bite back, thinking the risk to our comfort is greater than the promise of healing. After all, these relationships involve annoyances, trials, and sometimes out-and-out sacrifice for the good of the whole. True mutuality is a difficult prospect and can be scary.

However, when we can overcome our anxieties and become willing to enter into these relationships, we can learn to live in a more mutualistic and symbiotic way where we don't have power over one another but rather power with one another. We learn to live in ways that are mutually beneficial to one another, allowing each other to flourish in ways that were not previously possible when we were separated by our fear or discomfort. We may have to deal with the coarse tail of correction and the out-and-out sacrifice of some of our deeply held beliefs. However, when we agree to live in a more mutual world, we can begin to grow in ways we never imagined possible.

Inclusive communities are not simply communities that have made room at their table for Queer folks. They are communities that are willing to dismantle their table and rebuild something with the input and experience of Queer folks. Perhaps a better term for this kind of community is an *embracing community.* Embracing communities are those that seek not just to include Queer people but also want to learn and grow from us and with us. These communities understand that the perspective of Queer people has been shaped by the way we have walked in the world and that if we want to be more loving communities, we will honor the ways in which people have been harmed and have healed. Embracing communities are willing to realize the need for symbiotic healing and mutual reliance. They listen. They trust. They participate, and together we all thrive.

Listening

Communities wishing to embrace Queer individuals and their families have to learn to listen. Queer individuals have spent their lives swimming in the water of heteronormativity and gender norms. We are acutely aware of the arguments against our identities and have likely confronted those arguments time and time again in our quest to know and understand ourselves well. We understand the confusion that others may be experiencing and are able to speak to it if communities are willing to embrace and listen well.

It is remarkably hard for people to listen without an agenda, but this is the first step to really hearing what Queer folks have to say. Communities must put aside their own biases and really hear what we are saying. One of the most difficult hurdles to jump when it comes to being heard is overcoming what people think they know about the Queer experience. Because there has been so much misinformation about Queer people, the temptation to allow the blanks in knowledge and understanding to be filled by secondhand information is great. When Nia came out as transgender, one of the first questions asked by some was "Who abused you?" They had been taught a common narrative that transgender and homosexual people have developed a pathology rooted in abuse suffered as a child. This was not the case for Nia by any stretch of the imagination, but for those unwilling to listen, childhood abuse became an easy scapegoat for what they saw as Nia's "condition."

Without the ability to listen, it is easy to jump to conclusions about what should be done. The thought is often *what would this be like for me?* rather than *what has it been like for you?* This is a natural human tendency, especially when people don't understand something or it lies so far afield from their lived experiences. Listening to people becomes remarkably hard when hearing well involves sifting through cultural opinions on the topic and lived experiences that don't include Queer identity. Some people in Nia's life hold strong opinions about who she is as a trans woman and state those opinions often, without ever asking her a single question about her own lived experience.

Many people asked our close friends if we would stay married after Nia's transition. Those who were walking alongside us knew us well enough to say yes, we would, but those who didn't see us up close all the time interpreted our marriage through their own experiences, which was unfair to both us and them. We have a very unique love story that thankfully includes both our gender and sexual identities. We don't expect everyone to have that same experience, but it is remarkable how so many heterosexual couples had trouble understanding us because they overlaid their experience onto ours without asking us about our experience.

We understand that putting aside a lifetime of experience in order to listen and learn can be difficult. It takes a lot of discipline to not fall into old thought patterns and beliefs. Listening to someone's perspective without overlaying our own experiences is an act of meditation. When someone is willing to tell us who they are, it is our job to focus our energies on what they are saying, not what we think they are saying, or what we want them to say, or what we're going to say. Listening means just that—listening. We are so conditioned toward response that simply holding the space for someone to tell us who they are is difficult. It is a practice, and with practice, it becomes easier.

Often, communities want individuals to address their pinch points, those parts of Queer identity that make them feel uncomfortable. So instead of listening to Queer individuals and families, they come into conversation hoping or outright asking for their discomfort to be solved. This is not the job of the Queer individual or family. The job of the Queer individual or family is to live our lives as ourselves; the community member's job is to wrestle with their discomfort while listening to the reality of the lives being lived in front of them.

Our good friend Jen exemplifies this type of listening and wrestling with discomfort. When Nia came out to Jen initially, there was a pause, a visible discomfort. But out of all the people who responded to Nia's identity with their own discomfort, Jen owned her discomfort. Where others took that moment of discomfort and tried to transfer it directly to Nia to own and solve, Jen listened, took her discomfort on as her own, and went away from the conversation to sit with it. She didn't power through, trying to listen to Nia in the face of that discomfort, but she acknowledged it and didn't press into conversation further at that moment. On reentering the conversation about Nia's trans identity days later, Jen was able to communicate that any discomfort Nia had noticed should not be owned by Nia. Jen was able to ask thoughtful questions and actually listen to the responses. This story of life lived between Jen and Nia in this moment is a wonderful example of what owning our own thoughts, experiences, beliefs, and stories can look like while building community together.

JEN'S LEAN-IN: Nia's coming out was not something I could have predicted. When she revealed to me that she is transgender, I was stunned and confused and uncomfortable. I definitely had my own opinions, but I recognized that Nia didn't come to me for my two cents or my advice. In fact, nothing had actually been asked of me except to listen to her story. It seemed the wisest choice for me, as a friend who wanted to be supportive, was to work on sorting out my own feelings and thoughts before saying something that couldn't be unsaid.

My upbringing and faith background, which is similar to Nia's, maintained that at best, LGBTQ+ folks are "in sin," and at worst they are demon-possessed. Maybe somewhere on that spectrum was some kind of personality disorder or psychological challenge, but certainly no well-balanced, moral person with integrity could be transgender. But there I was, face to face with an individual I personally knew to be kind and honest and generous. The truth in front of me didn't align with what I'd been taught my whole life.

At the time, her transition felt like heavy, unwelcome, and very complicated news that I couldn't wrap my head around. I wanted to explain it away, so the easy choice would have been to write Nia off as confused or a sinner, but she didn't seem to be either. The one and only thing that was clear to me was that *I knew nothing* about being transgender, so I decided to challenge my discomfort by educating myself.

The first thing I did was go to my streaming service, and I typed in *transgender*. I started watching shows with transgender characters. Then I started following transgender people on social media. I read blogs and articles that were about gender fluidity or theology that affirmed LGBTQ+ people. I had never been exposed to this kind of information before, and I had never bothered to seek it out myself because it didn't seem relevant to my life or to me personally.

By the time I reached out to Nia again, I felt much more comfortable because of what I had watched and read. I knew she wasn't a pariah; she was still my friend. I tried to lead with curiosity and asked her, "May I ask you some questions?" She met my curiosity with openness, and we were able to begin a dialogue that was free from judgment on either side.

Because of our mutual respect and that foundation of honesty we had laid with our conversations, she also asked me questions that she may not have asked other friends. I remember being out one evening, and she asked me if I was comfortable enough to go to the public restroom together, as ladies sometimes do. I was able to answer very honestly and told her, "No, I'm not comfortable with that yet." She respected both my frankness and my preference to visit the restroom alone.

I'm very grateful that Nia was willing to talk about her own journey with me, and she tackled my questions with vulnerability. She did also set boundaries, so I knew there were some things that she wasn't willing to discuss with me, and I didn't push.

Ultimately, I knew my discomfort was my own, and what I did with it was up to me. It wasn't Nia's job to make me feel good or satisfied. Taking the posture of a learner was a very intentional choice for me, and I worked against decades of instruction and judgments I held. Had I not chosen to listen and learn, I may still be sitting in my own confusion, distress, and prejudice.

We can't do this if we are separate; we can only do this in relationship. If a community wants to move toward inclusion but works toward that goal from its own perspective, on its own terms, before entering relationships with its Queer folks, then it is being exploitative at worst and performative at best. We have seen this in communities that truly desire to be embracing but are unwilling to look beyond their current structures for change. Spaces such as these often end up wondering why their communities are not more diverse, and this is usually because attempts at diversity and inclusion are built inside of their existing system, instead of seeking genuine relationships that lead to systemic changes within the community. Without a mutual lived relationship, we cannot really hear each other and cannot truly be an embracing community.

Trusting

This kind of relational listening involves a great deal of trust. Communities have to be willing to believe what Queer folks are saying about our lived experiences without demanding proof or requiring long, drawn-out explanations. When we tell you who we are, you should believe us, not fight us on our own identity. To tell a Queer person that we are simply confused about our identity is incredibly disrespectful and, in fact, not our problem. The problem is rooted in the belief that you can know me better than I know myself—when in reality, nobody knows me better than I know me.

If we are to build embracing communities, we must learn to trust that each individual within the community knows themselves and their experiences. Trust should be our default setting, not something that is begrudgingly acquiesced to after enough proof has been presented. Imagine having to prove your identity to those around you over and over again. For many Queer folks, this is the reality. We are trained in many ways to prove the validity of our identities before we are allowed to share anything else about ourselves. This can be why it seems like Queer people only talk about being Queer or have to be so loud and sometimes angry about it. It's not because we have no other identifiers; it is because we are often forced to protect and defend the particularity of our Queerness. Communities that demand proof of the validity of people's Queer experiences are creating one-dimensional personalities because folks are forced to authenticate their sexual or gender experience above all else.

Trust is how we resist the urge to turn people into issues. Trust makes a flat, lifeless community come alive with robust energy. Trust propels us beyond our current understandings and opens our minds to new ideas and ways of being in the world. When our foundation with one another is trust, we have a firm anchor. Divisions arise where there is no trust. We have seen this in our world. It's hard to know where to go for correct information, to know who is telling us the truth. In this day of fake news, how do we know who has the answers? Our good friend and Queer seminarian Erin Sanzero once said to us, "God doesn't give us answers. God gives us each other."[2]

If communities wait until they have all the information they need to be embracing without trusting the Queer folks around them, we will never see robust communities of change. Our world cannot progress if we continually look for our answers outside of ourselves and our relationships with one another. Each of us holds a key to what a good, healthy community looks like. It's wrong to think that one person or group has all the answers. We have to trust that our understanding is limited based on our own experiences, and the only way to fill in those gaps is to learn from one another. You don't have to fully understand the experience of another to trust that what they are saying is true.

Participating

When we listen and trust one another, we can start to build communities based on all of our experiences and perspectives. This will require that Queer folks, and all historically marginalized and underrepresented people, have participation at every level of our community life, not just in visibility but in ideology and practice. Because Queer folks have lived life from a differing perspective, what they bring to a community is not just diversity in appearance but diversity of thought. It is important that embracing communities understand that by including Queer members in places of leadership, ingrained patterns of thinking and behaving will be challenged and will change.

One way in which communities disservice Queer people and themselves is by installing Queer folks into places of leadership as tokens. Tokens are individuals who represent an underrepresented group that are brought to the table for the expressed goal of diversity. However, when folks in these roles begin to deviate from the standard practice of the group or ask for deeper reflection based on a wider range of perspectives, the tokenized person is often shut down or told that they are asking for too much change.

Tokenizing an individual is an easy way to quiet those who want to be represented without changing the fundamentals of why that representation doesn't occur in the first place. Feminist philosopher and theologian Mary Daly said, "Tokenism does not change stereotypes of social systems but works to preserve them, since it dulls the revolutionary impulse."[3] If we want to see change in our world, we cannot settle for tokenism in our communities. We must push forward, listening and trusting the experiences of Queer people to reveal to us a fresh path.

In her address to a feminist conference in 1979, Black Queer feminist author and activist Audre Lorde summed up the ideas of communal participation by reminding a room of academic, mostly white feminists, "Community must not be a shedding of our differences, nor the pretense that those differences do not exist." Lorde chastised this community of elite feminists and asked them to challenge their tokenism of her by expressing just how important understanding the perspectives and experiences of all women were to the advancement of feminist ideology. She went on to say:

> Those of us who stand outside the circle of this society's definition of acceptable women; those of us who have been forged in the crucibles of difference; those of us who are poor, who are lesbians, who are black, who are older, know that survival is not an academic skill. It is learning

how to stand alone, unpopular, and sometimes reviled, and how to make common cause with those other identi-fied as outside the structures, in order to define and seek a world in which we can all flourish. It is learning how to take our differences and make them strengths. For the master's tools will never dismantle the master's house.[4]

Lorde pulls no punches as she asks us to "make common cause with those others identified as outside the structures." And she makes it clear that we will never see equality and inclusion if we are seeking to participate in the systems around us on their terms. If our communities are to be communities of radical love and change, we must learn to let go of the ways things have been done in the past. It is time to learn what it means to live in a community that isn't built from the same building blocks that resulted in the exclusion of Queer individuals and their families. If we are to build embracing communities, we have to acknowl-edge that our differences exist *and* they make us stronger when we work together in love.

Thriving

Our natural world is a world of change. Nature renews itself according to a familiar rhythm. Each season brings a new chal-lenge—sometimes death, sometimes new life. This is true for our human nature as well. Our world, our views, our laws are all constantly changing. Each generation brings with it a new ideol-ogy. We move forward together as a human race. Where we are going is up to us.

There will be seasons of change that are painful. It will feel as though we are dying. In many real and tangible ways, old ways of thinking and behaving will have to die. However, just as a snake must shed its too small skin and a hermit crab must find a new shell to fit its mature body, if we are growing, we will have to acknowledge our growth, release what no longer fits us, and look for new and larger containers for our love.

Our world can feel like a never-ending cycle of nightmarish hatred. It can be difficult to see the same old prejudices rear their heads generation after generation. We will take two steps forward and one step back. But the more we are willing to push into a new future, the more likely it is we will someday look around and realize we are in a completely different place. This is not something that we can do in isolation. Turning hearts toward hope is not a one-person job. It is the job of the community. That is why community exists—to bring us hope. Community is where we go to remind ourselves that we are not alone. It is where we are repaired and renewed because we are deeply loved and cared for. The community honors its members because it is nothing without them.

We believe Queer Afrofuturist novelist Octavia E. Butler when she says, "There is nothing new under the sun, but there are new suns."[5] The only way to discover a new way of being is to listen to those who have experienced life differently. If we desire a world where there is less division and more love, we will have to open our hearts to one another. We have to walk with one another and learn from each other. We will have to accept each other beyond the bounds of our understanding. We will have to trust in the deep goodness and beauty of each human being. We will have to live authentically and embrace our differences. Only then will we live in a world driven by unity rather than our division. When we embrace Queer families, we will find new suns.

TOOLKIT

The Journey of Pronouns

One of the difficult parts of coming out as trans, nonbinary, or genderfluid is helping others understand name and pronoun changes. For loved ones and family members, making the switch can be difficult because there are no good scripts. If our loved one has changed their name and pronouns and knows what they would like to use, it is our responsibility as someone they have entrusted with their identity to make that switch as quickly and concretely as we can. For those of us being let in on our loved one's journey toward a greater understanding of their gender identity, this can be more nuanced. Everyone around us may not know our loved one's new pronouns. Here are a few quick tips to help you navigate the journey of pronouns alongside your loved one who may not be ready to make the concrete switch to something new:

* Ask if they know what pronouns they would like to use.
* If they want to try on a new pronoun, give them space and provide them the opportunity to do that by using that pronoun in their presence.
* If they are unsure what pronoun they would like but don't want to use the pronoun assigned to them at birth, ask them if using *they/them* feels good. If not, ask if using their name instead of pronouns would be helpful

(i.e., I love spending time with Ainsley because Ainsley is so fun and vivacious. Ainsley really brings the party everywhere that Ainsley goes.). This may feel stilted and a little awkward, but it helps diffuse the need for pronouns when they are a source of strife.

✳ If your loved one is not ready to reveal a new pronoun in public, but you want to honor their choices, try utilizing the name technique above. Instead of using pronouns, simply use their name. It is remarkable how few people catch on when we simply omit or replace pronouns with our loved one's name.

✳ Take the time and effort to understand where your loved one is coming from and how pronouns make them feel. The more we understand about our loved one's journey, the easier it is to honor it.

✳ Understand that with this gender journey, your loved ones may switch pronouns more than once or be okay with you using more than one pronoun.

Make the Switch

When our loved one's coming out involves a change of name and/or pronouns, it is important that we make the switch to using their identifiers as early and often as we can. While it's easy to say we are trying, without concrete steps toward making changes, our loved one may not feel supported. Here are some quick ways you can make sure you are reminding yourself to honor your loved one:

✳ Change their contact information on your phone.
✳ Talk often with others who know about your loved one's identity and practice using their name and pronouns in conversation.

* If your loved one is still in school, help them get teachers and faculty on board with their name and pronouns.
* If you keep a journal or diary, switch the name and pronouns you use for your loved one.
* In any written communication, go out of your way to name your loved one and their pronouns.
* When thinking about your loved one, use their name and pronouns in your mind.
* When you are around your loved one, slow down. Our brains can rely on rote scripts, and to get outside of those, we must be deliberate and slower to speak.
* If your loved one is out, correct anyone around you who is using any other names and pronouns than what your loved one wishes.
* Try looking at memories of your loved one through the lens of their name and pronoun. Memories can be especially tricky, and people often don't know how to address someone who has transitioned in past tense. Our advice is to always err on the side of their current name and pronouns and have a deeper conversation on how they see themselves pre-transition.

Mantras for Boundary-Keeping

Boundaries are one of the most important tools we possess as we travel together on our journey toward living authentically. We have seen that one of the most difficult parts of holding boundaries is knowing what to say to ourselves when people breach those boundaries to remind ourselves why the boundary is important. This is especially the case when someone in our life repeatedly crosses our boundaries and tries, consciously or not, to subvert our boundaries in different ways, negotiating with our stated needs. In this case, we find it helpful to have personal mantras that remind us why we are holding any particular boundary.

One of the ways in which we determined if people were safe for our family after Nia's transition was by drawing a line in the sand that people would need to use her name and pronouns and/or be actively working toward using her name and pronouns, even if they failed and needed to correct themselves. There were those who asked to call her nothing at all, but our firm stance was that even dogs have names. We were not willing for Nia to be treated with less dignity than the family pet.

Knowing what we will and won't accept as we move through the coming-out journey together is essential to our healthy development, both individually and as a family. *Even dogs have names* became a mantra in our household to remember that we are worthy of being treated with respect and dignity. We encourage families to embrace mantras that make sense for you and remind you why you are making the boundaries you are. We also encourage those who are having trouble respecting boundaries to assess why it is so difficult to respect the wishes of your loved one and how you can move closer to honoring their boundaries in order to partake in a loving relationship based on honor and respect. Here are some examples of mantras you may want to adopt:

* I am worthy of love and respect.
* I don't owe others an explanation for who I am or whom I choose to love.
* I am allowed to honor my feelings and protect my heart when necessary.
* I belong to myself.
* I can trust myself.
* I deserve to have love and joy without guilt.

Scripts for Boundary-Setting

Mantras remind us of our worth to ourselves; scripts help us communicate our boundaries to others. If you encounter difficulty and need to set boundaries, here are a few scripts to have on hand. These statements are firm without being confrontational and allow you to express your needs without placing blame on the other.

* "I will not be discussing that aspect of my loved one's identity."
* "My position of support is not up for discussion."
* "Please do not try to process your emotions about my loved one's identity with me. I am focused on their growth and my own feelings right now. If you continue, I will have to leave this conversation."
* "I am not at liberty to say."
* "No."
* "I am choosing to trust my loved one with their own identity."
* "If you need support, I am happy to give you the name of a few resources, but I cannot be your primary resource at this time."
* "I respect that your position is different from mine, but I do not want to discuss it."

The Most Important Words We Can Learn

The most important words in our vocabulary as interdependent relational human beings are *I'm sorry* and, in return, *I forgive you*. These words can work wonders in moving relationships from places of rupture and pain toward healing and wholeness. All of us will need to learn these phrases and practice them liberally throughout the letting-in and coming-out process. They are equally important for us as individuals—being kind to ourselves and forgiving our own mistakes—and in our relationships when we hurt one another and are in need of forgiveness for our actions.

Many of us have very little practice in saying *I'm sorry* and even less in returning *I forgive you.* We are groomed for defensiveness, so we invite you to practice saying these words out loud on a daily basis to familiarize yourself with them. If you live alone, take notice of times when you make mistakes. Maybe you overslept your alarm, making your morning routine hectic, forgetting breakfast, and realizing you don't have any deodorant on in the car on the way to work. For many of us, this can send our day reeling because we are so upset with ourselves we can't get past it and on with our day. We spend the day internally berating ourselves for not having our shit together.

In this instance, we recommend taking a timeout in your car, taking a deep breath, and telling yourself, "I'm sorry. I hit the snooze button one too many times this morning, and I got worked up over my mistake. I'm sorry, self. I'm going to set the alarm for five minutes earlier tonight." This act of telling ourselves we're sorry is a great first step in loving ourselves well. We don't have to beat ourselves up by saying, "Oh, yeah, you stupid idiot, you better set that alarm earlier, but I know you're gonna forget, dummy." Instead, we can say, "I forgive you, self. I'll make a calendar reminder to set the alarm for five minutes earlier as soon as I get in the office. Or better yet, Siri, make a note." We can love ourselves well by taking immediate steps to forgive our mistakes and work on doing it better the next time. We may also want to throw some deodorant in our glove box.

If you live with a partner and/or with children, there are a million times in a day to practice saying *I'm sorry*. Some examples might be:

* "Hey, bud, I'm sorry I yelled this morning when we were late. I was feeling rushed, and I was frustrated. I am so sorry for yelling. Can you forgive me?" / "I forgive you, Mom. I will try to get in the car on time tomorrow."
* "I'm sorry I didn't take the trash out last night. I completely forgot. I will set a reminder on my phone for next time." / "I forgive you, and I took the trash out for you. Thanks for setting a reminder."
* "I'm sorry I said the wrong pronoun. *'She* said that *she* was looking forward to *her* birthday." / "I forgive you. Thanks for correcting yourself."

While saying sorry does not always result in forgiveness, apologizing does go a long way, especially when combined with a strategy for change. There are so many ways in which we will mess up when a loved one comes out. Whether it's saying the wrong pronoun, breaching boundaries, reverting to past expectations, or behaving poorly when we meet our loved one's partner, when we make mistakes and don't acknowledge them, we drive a wedge between ourselves and our loved ones. However, when we are able to name our offenses, own them, and pledge to do better, we can work toward a healthier relationship.

The same is true for forgiveness. Withholding forgiveness from a penitent person does nothing but cause us great angst and bitterness. If we find we are having trouble forgiving a genuine person, we should seek counsel from a trusted friend or therapist to discover the deeper wound hiding behind the situation. It may hurt to find the reason forgiveness is so difficult. However, the work we do to uncover our hesitations can help inform what we need out of our relationships going forward.

As Maya Angelou says, "When you know better, you do better."[1] This is what life is about. We will never get it right all the time, so we have to be willing to do the work of saying *I'm sorry.* In the same way, when we are gracious with others, we learn to be gracious with ourselves. When we say, "I forgive you," in many ways we are saying we love each other, and we make room for us all to belong.

Calling In versus Calling Out

We live in a culture that is ripe for division partly because of our growing freedoms to embrace who we are. Widespread use of the internet as well as social media allows us to be able to see others, hear their opinions, and voice ours like no other time in history. While this has led to major advances in organizing and recognition of harms, such as the #MeToo movement, it has also led to realization of the deep chasm that exists among people's lived experiences. Rightfully so, we are now able to hold people accountable for the things they say and do at a rate and speed never before possible. What we see now is a deepening of division when we are quick to call people out without calling them in.

When we call someone out, holding them accountable for their actions with no way of seeking forgiveness and offering restitution, we are pinning them into a box and closing the lid. It is good and right for people to be held accountable for their actions and words. However, if there is no way for them to learn and grow from their mistakes, we risk a deepening anger and resentment that will likely lead to an even more egregious act. Calling out someone without also calling them in leaves too much room for blame in the wrong direction.

On the other hand, when we call someone into conversation, we come to them with the assumption of positive intent, meaning we assume they don't know what they are saying or doing. This stance helps us to prevent projecting our anger onto the person. When someone genuinely asks us, "Do you have a wife?" just because we're a man or asks an invasive question such as "Have you had bottom surgery?" pulling them aside and pointing out how their words and actions impacted you can be more effective than calling them out on social media or in front of a crowd. Our good friend Kristin taught us this when she heard Nia use a common phrase that had racial undertones Nia was not aware of. She decided instead of blasting Nia for using the word, she would text Nia and let her know that what was said could be construed as an insult and gave options for better words to use in the future. Instead of becoming angry and digging in her heels, Nia thanked Kristin for letting her know as she'd never want to purposefully harm someone. Instead of Kristin's actions driving a wedge between her and Nia, her ability to call her in was the beginning of their friendship, which is now deep and strong.

Since learning this technique from Kristin, we have used it repeatedly with, admittedly, varying degrees of success. It is true that some people don't like being wrong in any way and take any criticism as an affront to themselves personally. When this is the case, we find no amount of conversation or argument will change their minds. It is better to let these people learn in a different way other than sacrificing our time and resources trying to convince them to change. By and large, however, we have found that people, while initially embarrassed, are more than willing to change their actions and language once they know someone is being negatively affected by their actions.

Having been called in ourselves, we find it is the best way to grow and learn. We are grateful for those who have taken the time to lovingly guide us. Our culture is so thoroughly steeped in racist and misogynist terminology that it is almost impossible to simply know and understand the origins of every offensive word or phrase. That is why relationships are so important: they help us become better versions of ourselves by simply loving each other well enough to call each other into difficult conversations.

Privacy versus Secrecy

For those of us living in the in-between moments of letting in and coming out, we can feel like we are holding a big secret. This was difficult for us as we had been taught that secrets were cousins of lies and therefore not acceptable. Katie had an especially difficult time with this distinction between secrets and lies until she was able to reframe this "secret" as something we simply needed to keep private.

Our gender and sexual identities are extremely personal and in some ways deeply private. Not everyone needs access to all the information about us at all times, especially when we are in the vulnerable space of discovering our identity and exploring how we want to express ourselves to the world. When we didn't grow up with or don't have a lot of privacy, this kind of protection can feel like we are hiding something. But we really aren't. It is essential that we are each able to confide in others according to our needs and desires at the time and expect that our vulnerability will be held in confidence.

This became especially important when letting our kids in on Nia's identity. We were not ready for the wider world to know Nia's gender identity, but our children could not help but notice shifts in her appearance around the house. Nia wanted to be freer to be herself in her own space, so it became necessary to have a conversation with our children about Nia's identity. We were also in the tender time of parenting when we were teaching our children about consent, safety, and what is and isn't appropriate for an adult to ask them to do. One of those things we conveyed as not appropriate was another adult asking them to keep a secret from us, their parents. And in this case, while it was us, their parents, asking them to hold confidence, we didn't feel comfortable asking them to keep Nia's identity a secret.

In order to alleviate conflating secrecy that can lead to harm with privacy, we first set up safe people for our children to talk to about Nia's identity outside of the two of us. Because we had created our circle of safety and identified our stars, we were able to tell our children that if they needed to discuss Nia's identity with anyone, they could go to these trusted adults. While we're not sure any of our kids took us up on this offer, it did diffuse the idea that this was a secret and instead was a private conversation to be had with safe adults.

Finding safe people to discuss who we are and what we are going through is so important. When we understand that what we are inviting people into isn't the keeping of a secret but entrusting someone with our vulnerability so we can grow in private, it helps lessen the weight we all feel we are carrying.

We can all benefit from understanding that privacy is a right that is due to all people. In this way, we can be safe in our more unguarded moments knowing that those who love us will treat our growth with care and tenderness.

Coming Out to Younger Kids

When Nia came out to our kids, they were all below the age of ten. We feared that her transgender identity would be a difficult concept for them to understand, but we also knew it was important for them to be a part of Nia's journey from as early as possible. It was important to us that our children were able to gradually familiarize themselves with Nia's female identity, so we decided we wanted to tell them sooner rather than later. We have a very open relationship with our children, so sitting down to talk to them about gender and sexuality was not odd to them.

It was important that when we came to the conversation, we were both on the same page. We already knew what our next steps were as a family, where we were going as a couple, and that our children may ask us questions we could not foresee. We decided that we would be able to field any concerns about our marriage and the fate of our family, and anything we didn't know we could learn together. We had already built a circle of safety so that when our kids needed additional processing, there were individuals they knew were safe to talk to who weren't either of us but could answer their questions and hold their concerns.

To simplify the idea of gender identity for our kids, Katie created a chart like the one below:

The chart laid out bodies and identity in terms of a spectrum, with one end of the spectrum being a male body with a

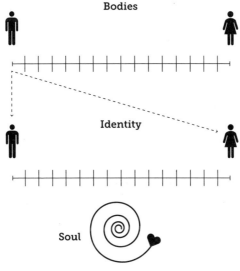

Figure 9: Gender Identity

male identity and the other being a female body with a female identity. We explained how people are not just their bodies, but they are also souls living in their bodies who deserve to see what is on the inside reflected on the outside. This was also a great opportunity to talk to our kids about intersex individuals, and that not all people have a biologically discernible sex, as well as nonbinary and gender-expansive individuals. While rudimentary, the chart provided a visual context for our children to understand what we were talking about as we explained that Nia's identity is female, she had been born into a male body, and that she wanted her outside to match her inside. We also outlined Katie's identity, that her body matched her identity, and asked our kids to explain where they might see themselves on the spectrum.

The resulting conversation was beautiful and surprising. Even our young kids understood what was being said to them, asked questions, and identified things about themselves they'd never given voice to before. Of course, Nia's transition would yield more questions, but starting in a safe conversation with openness and curiosity allowed our kids to feel comfortable and own their experience of her transition.

A few months after this interaction, Katie was playing outside with the kids, and our daughter mentioned a teacher was changing her name the next semester because she was getting married. Katie asked her how long she thought it would take for kids to get used to saying their teacher's new name. Our son piped up that he thought everyone would get it right away, but our daughter took a moment to think about it and responded that it would probably take about three months for the kids to get used to their teacher using a new name, approximately the same amount of time it had been since our conversation about Nia's transition. It was clear to Katie that our daughter was feeling out if it was okay that it was taking some time for her to get used to Nia's transition and also asking for patience because kids take time to adjust.

Our eldest kids are now teenagers, and we recently had a discussion about their feelings during the early days of Nia's transition. They were very open and honest about the ways in which they were affected and expressed that they felt that while it wasn't exactly easy, difficult emotions such as fear and disappointment came and went as we moved forward together as a family. Our family encountered many changes during Nia's transition that affect all of us, both now and in the future. However, it is clear that our kids are thriving in a family that supports them, honors their experiences, and provides safety and love.

Create Curiosity

One of the most important tools in resiliency is curiosity. When we are curious about our world and teach our children to be curious, we become people who are open-minded, and we learn to see our circumstances as opportunities for growth and learning. Unwillingness to dive into curiosity can leave us feeling frustrated, cheated, and stuck. However, when we are willing to ask questions and investigate, we can discover not only beautiful truths about what and who surrounds us but we can also dig deeper into the reality of who we are and all that we have to offer the world. Love is a curiosity that will continually teach us if we are prepared.

Physicist Neil deGrasse Tyson exemplifies cultivating this kind of curiosity with his daughter, as he explained during an appearance on *The Late Show with James Corden.*[2] Neil's daughter had started losing her teeth and asked her dad if the tooth fairy was real. Instead of answering his daughter directly, deGrasse Tyson simply asked her, "What do you think?" This led to a series of experiments within their home and the eventual recruitment of her friends at school to find out if the tooth fairy was indeed real. Although his daughter and her classmates discovered the truth about the tooth fairy, through this experimentation, he gave his daughter the gift of agency as well as understanding.

deGrasse Tyson also makes a point to remind us that the universe is magnificent enough without having to make things up and adds another layer of beauty to curiosity: awe and magic. There is nothing wrong with believing in the tooth fairy; in fact, it is part of the magic of childhood. Recognizing the magic, understanding that we can choose into that belief, and still integrating that wonder into our lives is what makes childhood rich and invites us into the adult world with our sense of play intact. Discovering through curiosity allows us to remain resilient.

The best way to begin cultivating this kind of curiosity is to lean into the lesson of the tooth fairy. When our children begin to ask us questions, we can respond, "What do you think?" In this way, we honor that our children have the capacity for reason and the capabilities to find their own answers.

Cultivating curiosity doesn't end with children; it is also something we can and should grow within ourselves as adults. By applying lessons from the tooth fairy, we can give ourselves permission to investigate the world around us. Too often we accept what is given to us at face value. We may have learned from a young age to stop asking *why* so much, but it's time to reclaim that innocence and naïveté and feed the curiosity that lives within us. This is how we grow and evolve as a human species and how we learn to become more loving.

Rewrite the Scripts

Our cultures are full of expectation, and two of the most common and increasingly complicated categories of expectation are gender and sexual identity. For generations, we have fallen into scripts regarding gender, sexuality, and family life that roll off our tongues without a second thought. However, if we want to create welcoming environments for everyone, then we need to rethink the way we speak. This is not only for the sake of those growing up in gender-diverse and sexually diverse identities but for all of us who need a broader, less restrictive view of what it means to be a fulfilled human being.

Simple language shifts can help create a more inclusive landscape for us all. Here are some examples to help jumpstart a new lexicon for conversation around gender, sexuality, and family life:

Instead of . . .	. . . try
"Got any boyfriends?"	"Tell me about your friends and anyone special in your life."
"When you are a dad, you will . . . "	"If you choose to have kids, what kind of parent do you want to be?"
"Your future wife" "Your future husband"	"Your future partner, if you choose to have one"

We don't have to scrub all gendered language or stop asking our loved ones about their plans or dreams for the future. However, we can choose to be aware that not all people encounter life in the same way or grow at the same rate. We may have children, friends, and relatives, some of whom we think we know very well, who identify in ways we are unaware of because our assumptions have left no room for conversation around who they are. There are many reasons young men don't have girlfriends or our child-free neighbors don't have kids. When we have spent our whole lives steeped in the scripts that tell us something is wrong because their reality doesn't match our vernacular, we jump to conclusions about how they should feel about themselves and unwittingly project our identities onto others.

If we are careful about our language, we are able to more readily listen to others when they express to us who they are. By opening our scripts to more inclusive ways of speaking, we allow others the opportunity to fill in their life experiences with what is important to them. In this way, we show our friends and family that we value who they are, and we are able to express who we are in kind.

Make Room for Defense

Before Nia came out, she was unsure how she would deal with the world's reaction to her being a transgender person. Her therapist mentioned early on that she should let her kids defend her. At the time, Nia didn't fully understand this, but after coming out, she saw that her kids regularly stood up for her. This was a joy and help as standing up for yourself in the face of misgendering, misnaming, microaggressions, or hate can be exhausting. And this isn't just a task for our children but for everyone in our circles of support. These folks can defend us while we are present or even if we aren't. Here are a few tips for coming to the defense of Queer individuals:

* As someone who is defending a Queer individual, you may want to use some of the following scripts:
   o "Can I tell you how that comment might be perceived by [Queer individual]?"
   o "I don't think you're trying to be hurtful here, but this is what it sounds like to me."
   o "I'm going to stop you right there. I'm not / we aren't going to engage in this type of conversation."
   o "Her name is Nia" (used when correcting names and pronouns).
* If you are someone who has made a mistake with names or pronouns or have been informed that something you said was offensive, apologize quickly—don't overdo it—correct your speech if necessary, and if needed, ask to

have a conversation later in order to understand your mistake better.

* As a Queer individual, if you are with someone who is affirming of you, don't immediately speak or react after something harmful is said in your presence. This allows an affirming friend who is with us to make corrections to what was said and to defend our identity where required. Also have the conversation with affirming friends up front about how they can best defend you when necessary.

Make Friends as an Individual and as a Family

As Nia came out, much of the community that we had built around us started to change. We had to find new places, spaces, and people who would support us in our Queer identity as well as in everyday life. While we drew closer to some of the people who were already in our lives, there were times when we needed to find new community. Many times, this requires a proactive approach. Here are some tips for branching out and finding new community:

* Reach out to a Queer organization near you for information on what activities may be available for someone like yourself, such as Queer sports leagues, Queer family events, and so on.

* Go to explicitly Queer spaces like restaurants owned by Queer people.

* Go to implicitly Queer spaces. Use Google searches such as "LGBTQ-friendly theater" or "LGBTQ-friendly restaurant" and look for the *LGBTQ-friendly* descriptor to find inclusive spaces.

✳ Be proud of who you are. When we live our lives authentically, we draw people to us who love us for who we are.

What Affirming Looks Like

When Nia came out, she did it via email in many cases. A few of the email responses she received stood out as good examples of what it looks like to affirm someone in their identity. When responding to someone who is letting you in or coming out to you, remember the following as you respond either in writing or in person:

1. **Don't respond with emotion.** If you find yourself in an emotional state, wait to write a response or let your loved one know you need some time and will come back to them soon.

2. **Think about the future.** Too many times, we say something to our loved one that we might regret later on down the road. Usually these things are said out of emotion so, again, walk away or take a beat. If we do say something we didn't mean, utilize the most important words, *I'm sorry.*

3. **Respond to what is written or said to you.** Sometimes we have a tendency to read into things that are said to us or overlay our stories on top of someone else's story when it's being shared with us. Don't. Simply respond to what was said.

4. **Respond with positive words and phrases and without invasive questions.** For a first response, saying things

like "I'm so happy for you" and "I'd like to support you in any way I can" is appropriate. Don't ask questions like "Will you be able to ever have kids?" or "Will you have surgery?" These types of questions may come down the road if you have a close relationship with someone but are not inside the anatomy of a good response.

5. **Don't say things you can't know.** When a loved one tells us about their Queer identity and relays struggles they are having in their lives, don't respond with phrases that we can't know if they are true or not. Phrases like "I'm sure they'll come around" or "I know you'll be fully supported at work" should be avoided.

6. **Love wins.** When in doubt, a loving response always wins. Say *I love you* without *but*s. "I love you, but it's going to take me some time" may be an honest response, but just stop at the "I love you" and return to the conversation. If you are not affirming, avoid a knee jerk *I love you*. Take some time to reflect and return to your loved one for a productive conversation, showing love through actions at all times.

Below are some examples of fantastic responses that were sent to Nia when she came out; these are used with permission. Feel free to use them as templates where appropriate.

Hi, Nia,

I just read the letter that was sent out this morning and wanted to send you a note of support. I'm so happy that you are able to live as your authentic self and wish you all the best throughout your transition. What a great example you are for all of us. I admire your openness and thank you for sharing your experience!

Hi, Nia,

    I'm so happy to hear you are more you today than you were yesterday. May that trend continue and may you feel supported along the way. I'm so happy for you and support you endlessly.

Hi, Nia,

    I'm proud to work for a company that is open and supportive and making space for everyone to be who they are. I hope you feel love and support from our team. Thanks for being brave and being you.

Rituals

A Ritual for Coming Out

An Altar in the World

Coming out will look different for everyone, and we believe it should be a time of celebration. At your initial coming out, you may feel like you want to celebrate in a large way with a party or gathering. You may also want to acknowledge your coming out in a more intimate way. Whatever you choose, know that you are worthy of love and celebration. Additionally, as we've noted, coming out is not always a one-time event. It may be that you find yourself coming out many times. One way to mark these occasions and remind yourself of your own inherent worth is to have something to return to, a sort of anchor for who you are and how you want to walk in this world.

    In many religious traditions, altars are a way that people remind themselves of what they believe, and they use them to mark changes or rituals in their lives. While a physical altar may not be what you need, we encourage you to make a mental altar, or memory, that you can return to when you need encouragement and reminder of who you are. Your ritual can be performed individually or with a small or large group of supportive people. We encourage you to make it your own. Here is an example of an altar in the world:

What you will need:

* A candle
* A journal
* A representational object—we recommend a small rock or crystal you can hold in your hand
* A prepared statement of your identity

What you will do:

* Gather your friends or quiet yourself in a moment of peaceful reflection.
* Light the candle and honor the space that you are providing yourself to be heard and loved in this moment.
* Hold your object in your hand, feeling the weight, size, and shape of it.
* Read aloud your prepared statement of your identity and allow yourself to feel the emotions connected to speaking your truth out loud.
* If you are practicing this ritual with others, allow them to speak words of affirmation over you.
* Take a final deep breath together and blow out the candle, signifying an end to the ritual.
* When you have the time, write down reflections of your experience in your journal.
* Place your object where you will see or feel it regularly to remind you of this moment.

Ritual for Grief

While the grief caused by the coming out of a loved one may be ambiguous and have little to no closure, we can give ourselves relief by allowing the acknowledgment of loss and the acceptance of and readiness for a new path.

CORD-CUTTING CEREMONY

One ancient ritual for detaching and moving forward is a cord-cutting ceremony. Cord-cutting allows us the same kind of autonomy we receive at birth with the cutting of the umbilical cord. Just as a baby begins to breathe on their own and survive outside the womb when the umbilical cord is severed, we can begin to create new paths by releasing our attachment to what has been and readying ourselves for what is to come.

We would like to note that although cord-cutting ceremonies have become common in both religious and secular contexts, they have roots in African and Indigenous practices. We acknowledge these roots and are thankful for the preservation of such a beautiful metaphor in the form of practice.

What you will need:

* ✳ Any sort of thick cord
* ✳ Scissors
* ✳ Candle*
* ✳ Journal*

*Optional

What you will do:
Cord-cuttings can be done on your own or with a friend. When we were ready for our own cord-cutting, we asked a local Reiki practitioner who is also a dear friend to craft a ceremony for us.

A brief Google search can help you find a cord-cutting guide, or you can ask a trusted friend to say a few words. It's also more than fine to perform this ritual on your own.

* Set up your space so you can be comfortable and uninterrupted. You may choose to light a candle, wrap up in a blanket, or even draw yourself a bath, however you feel most at home. Have your cord and scissors close at hand.
* Take time to reflect on what you are grieving through meditation, prayer, or journaling. You may want to have a friend read through a poem that you love or spend some time talking about fond memories. It is important to remember we are not erasing our past but releasing ourselves from its control over our future.
* When you feel as though you are ready to release your attachment to what you are grieving, use the scissors to cut the cord. At the same time, allow yourself to imagine your own attachment to your past coming undone. Notice how both ends of the cord still exist, just as your past and your future still exist. Each simply lives on its own now, without pulling on the other.
* Take time to reflect on your feelings through meditation, prayer, or journaling. If you are practicing with a friend, allow them to speak words of encouragement over you.
* Inhale and exhale, acknowledging that the ache of grief still exists. However, it does not control you. You are free to move forward.

Ritual for Belonging

Once you have established a few members of your circle of safety, ask if they would be willing to sit with you as you breathe in the fresh air of love. If there are enough of you, sit in the center of the circle and allow your friends to surround you. If there are multiple people discovering support, such as in a support group, form a circle together. If you feel comfortable, you can hold hands or have your friends place their hands on you. Choose a song that you love or has particular meaning for you and have one friend lead you through the following:

* Say, "This is a group of healing and welcome, where we all belong exactly as we are. We support you (or each other) as you move through your journey."
* Take three deep breaths together as a group.
* Play the song that you have chosen and listen together.
* Take three deep breaths together as a group.
* Say, "As we leave this circle, may we carry with us the strength that it represents. May your heart be fortified. May you always know that you belong."

Ritual for Celebrating Queer Family

LET'S PARTY!

When a loved one comes out and we want to support them, the best thing to do is celebrate. However your family celebrates significant life events; it's time to throw a party.

When Nia turned forty, we knew we wanted a big blowout. It just so happened that her fortieth birthday fell right around the time we were preparing for a cross-country move. We decided to have a huge going-away party with all of our friends and family who had seen us through her transition journey. We also decided it was the perfect time to renew our vows as a couple with a surprise wedding. Nia bought a wedding gown, we asked our good friends to officiate, and we threw a giant party. Our house is now littered with pictures from our second wedding, serving as a reminder of all we've been through and all that we are as a family. We catered the experience exactly as we wanted it to be and celebrated who we are as a family together with our closest circles of support. It was magical.

For your celebration, think about the following:

* Who is important to have present?
* What do we most want to celebrate?
* How can we make each member of our family feel special and significant?
* How can we appropriately honor our Queer family member?

The rest is up to you. Let's party, y'all. We deserve it!

Ritual for Communal Invitation

GARDEN MANDALA

When your community is ready to mark its journey into becoming a place of peace, set aside some time to gather together and create a temporary art piece.

What you will need:

* A large open space
* A rough outline of what you would like to create
* Several extra flowers, rocks, or sticks for community members who may not have them
* A special song
* A prepared statement

What you will do:

* Ask your community members to each bring a flower, rock, plant, stick, or other natural material to your next

gathering. Make sure you have extra for members who may not have resources.

* Roughly mark out the design you would like to make on the ground using chalk or light-colored spray paint.
* Gather community members together and deliver your prepared statement or have members of your community bring statements they would like to share about the affirming and inclusive place of peace you are making as a community.
* As you play a special song, have community members lay their materials on your design until it is filled and colorful.

While your physical mandala will be temporary, the symbolic nature of your dedication to affirmation will be remembered by your community members. You can use this mandala as a touch point as your community lives and grows. The mandala ritual can also become an annual event rededicating your community to inclusivity and welcoming new members.

RESOURCE LIST

The resources below are intended to assist in the journey in and journey out, for both individuals and families. In times of crisis, helplines and mental health resources should be utilized. All resources may not be right for everyone, and each person should vet and understand an organization before getting involved or utilizing its services.

* Advocates for Youth—Advocates for Youth works alongside thousands of young people here in the United States and around the globe as they fight for sexual health, rights, and justice.
  * **LGBTQ+ Resources and Tools** https://www.advo catesforyouth.org/resources-tools/?_sft_audience= for-professionals
  * **Are You an Askable Parent?** https://www.advocates foryouth.org/resources/health-information/are -you-an-askable-parent/
* American Psychological Association (APA)—The leading scientific and professional organization representing psychology in the United States, with more than 146,000 researchers, educators, clinicians, consultants, and students as its members.

- ○ **Just the Facts about Sexual Orientation** (use the search bar to search for other resources) https://www.apa.org/pi/lgbt/resources/just-the-facts
- ○ **Understanding Sexual Orientation and Homosexuality** https://www.apa.org/topics/lgbtq/orientation

✳ American School Counselor Association (ASCA)—Supports school counselors' efforts to help students focus on academic, career, and social/emotional development so they achieve success in school and are prepared to lead fulfilling lives as responsible members of society.
- ○ **Position on Trans and Gender-Nonconforming Youth** https://schoolcounselor.org/Standards-Positions/Position-Statements/ASCA-Position-Statements/The-School-Counselor-and-Transgender-Gender-noncon

✳ American Veterans for Equal Rights (AVER)—Founded in 1990, AVER is made up of active service members, retirees, and reserve members advocating for the equal treatment of all members of the military, including LGBTQ+ individuals who are often oppressed by military policies. AVER has chapters throughout the United States to ensure strong support in each region. https://aver.us/

✳ Bisexual Resource Center (BRC)—BRC is a nonprofit organization dedicated to raising awareness of bisexuality and advocating for bisexual visibility. Because bisexual individuals are discriminated against by both heterosexuals and other members of the LGBTQ+ community, BRC aims to provide support and work toward a world where everyone is celebrated. https://biresource.org/

✳ <u>Center for Disease Control (CDC)</u>—CDC is the nation's leading science-based, data-driven service organization that protects the public's health. For more than seventy years, they've put science into action to help children stay healthy so they can grow and learn.
   ○ **LGBTQ+ Youth Resources** https://www.cdc.gov /lgbthealth/youth-resources.htm
✳ <u>CenterLink</u>—CenterLink's database contains information about member LGBT Community Centers and member affiliates in the United States and around the world.
   ○ **Directory of LGBTQ Centers** https://www .lgbtqcenters.org/LgbtCenters
✳ <u>*Disclosure* (Documentary Film)</u>—*Disclosure* is an unprecedented, eye-opening look at transgender depictions in film and television, revealing how Hollywood simultaneously reflects and manufactures our deepest anxieties about gender.
✳ <u>*Embracing the Journey* (Book by Greg and Lynn McDonald)</u>—A sympathetic, compassionate, and inspiring guide for parents from the founders of one of the first Christian ministries for parents of LGBTQ+ children.
✳ <u>Family Acceptance Project</u>—The Family Acceptance Project® (FAP) has developed the first online resource for diverse LGBTQ+ youth and families to help decrease mental health risks and promote well-being. https:// familyproject.sfsu.edu/
   ○ **Youth and Family Services** https://familyproject .sfsu.edu/youth-family-services
✳ <u>Family Equality</u>—Founded in 1979 at the National March on Washington for Lesbian and Gay Rights, Family Equality has spent more than forty years ensuring

that everyone has the freedom to find, form, and sustain their families by advancing equality for the LGBTQ+ community. https://familyequality.org/

✳ Forge—Forge dedicates its resources to building resilience in the transgender community. The organization offers training and resources to help family, friends, and professionals support transgender individuals in a respectful way. Forge also has resources available on building healthy relationships as a transgender individual, having positive interactions with community members, and supporting transgender healthcare. https://forge-forward.org/

✳ Gay and Lesbian Alliance Against Defamation (GLAAD)—Founded in 1985, GLAAD advocates for the acceptance of all LGBTQ+ individuals by working with media organizations to ensure that television shows, news coverage, and advertising promote acceptance and discourage discrimination. GLAAD has also organized national marches and other events to increase awareness of important issues in the LGBTQ+ community. https://www.glaad.org/

✳ Gay, Lesbian and Straight Education Network (GLSEN)—GLSEN works to ensure that LGBTQ+ students are able to learn and grow in a school environment free from bullying and harassment.
  ○ **Educator Resources** http://live-glsen-website.panthe onsite.io/resources/educator-resources

✳ Genders and Sexualities Alliance (GSA) Network—The GSA Network consists of student-led chapters at middle schools and high schools throughout the United States. Chapter members work to promote social change and increase the acceptance of youths of all orientations and identities. The GSA Network also has virtual chapters to ensure LGBTQ+ students can stay connected even when they're not in school.

o **Information on How to Register/Start a GSA** https://gsanetwork.org/gsa-registration/

* *God and the Gay Christian* (Book by Matthew Vines)— The landmark book exploring what the Bible actually says—and doesn't say—about same-sex relationships.

* Healthy Children—Healthy Children is run by the American Academy of Pediatrics (AAP) and its member pediatricians who dedicate their efforts and resources to the health, safety, and well-being of infants, children, adolescents, and young adults. Healthychildren.org

o **Coming Out: Information for Parents of LGBTQ+ Teens** https://www.healthychildren.org /English/ages-stages/teen/dating-sex/Pages/Four -Stages-of-Coming-Out.aspx

* Human Rights Campaign (HRC)—The Human Rights Campaign strives to end discrimination against LGBTQ+ people and realize a world that achieves fundamental fairness and equality for all.

o **LGBTQ+ Youth Resources** https://www.hrc.org /resources/lgbtq-youth

o **Creating Safe and Welcoming Schools** https:// welcomingschools.org/

* It Gets Better Project—The mission of the It Gets Better Project is to empower LGBTQ+ youths and remind them that they're not alone. What started out as a social media campaign is now a global platform that brings LGBTQ+ youths together and promotes acceptance of every sexual orientation and gender identity. https://itgetsbetter.org/

* <u>KidsHealth</u>—Nemours® KidsHealth® was founded in 1995. Since then, Nemours KidsHealth articles, videos, animations, print publications, and health instructions have had billions of visits. Nemours KidsHealth is the most-viewed site for dependable information on children's health, behavior, and development from before birth through the teen years.
    o Sexual Orientation https://www.kidshealth.org/en /parents/sexual-orientation.html
* <u>Lambda Legal</u>—For more than five decades, Lambda Legal has been working to change laws, policies, and minds so that LGBTQ+ Americans and everyone living with HIV can live with full equality. https://lambdalegal .org/
* <u>Love in the Face</u>—Support for transgender and LGBTQ+ individuals and families. https://www.lovein theface.com/
* <u>National Center for Lesbian Rights (NCLR)</u>—With a commitment to racial and economic justice, the NCLR promotes equal rights for LGBTQ+ individuals. Members work to influence public policy and educate the public on some of the key issues faced by members of the LGBTQ+ community. When necessary, the NCLR files lawsuits to remedy situations involving discrimination. https://www.nclrights.org/
* <u>National Center for Transgender Equality (NCTE)</u>— NCTE works to increase the acceptance of transgender individuals and influence policy so that members of the transgender community can work, attend school, and participate in community activities without fear of discrimination. The organization emphasizes equal

opportunity and access to healthcare, safety, and justice as part of its mission. https://transequality.org/

✳ National Center on Safe Supportive Learning Environments—The National Center on Safe Supportive Learning Environments is funded by the US Department of Education, Office of Elementary and Secondary School's Office of Safe and Supportive Schools. The center offers information and technical assistance to states, districts, schools, institutions of higher education, and communities focused on improving school climate and conditions for learning.

○ **Lessons from the Field—Supporting Transgender and Nonbinary Students in K–12 Schools** https://safesupportivelearning.ed.gov/events/webinar/lessons-field-supporting-transgender-nonbinary-students-k-12-schools

✳ National Council on Family Relations (NCFR)—NCFR is the premier professional association for understanding families through interdisciplinary research, theory, and practice.

○ **Support Resources for LGBTQ Individuals and Families** https://www.ncfr.org/resources/resource-collections/support-resources-lgbtq-individuals-and-families

✳ National LGBTQ Task Force—The National LGBTQ Task Force is an advocacy group that works to make sure LGBTQ+ individuals have equal access to freedom and justice. Activists work to end discrimination and eliminate barriers for the LGBTQ+ community when it comes to healthcare, employment, housing, retirement, and other aspects of life. https://www.thetaskforce.org

✳ <u>Our Family Coalition</u>—Advances equity for LGBTQ+ families with children through support, education, and advocacy. https://ourfamily.org/

✳ <u>Out and Equal</u>—Out and Equal is the premier organization working exclusively on LGBTQ+ workplace equality. Through its worldwide programs, Fortune 500 partnerships, and annual Workplace Summit conference, it helps LGBTQ+ people thrive and support organizations creating a culture of belonging for all. https://outandequal.org/

✳ <u>Parents, Families and Friends of Lesbians and Gays (PFLAG)</u>—PFLAG is an organization dedicated to ensuring that all people are valued and respected. Membership is open to LGBTQ+ individuals, their family members, and allies advocating for equal rights. PFLAG has active chapters throughout the United States, making it a good source of support in your community. https://pflag.org/

✳ <u>Queer Grace</u>—An online encyclopedia for LGBTQ+ and Christian life. http://queergrace.com/

✳ <u>Stand with Trans</u>—Stand with Trans is saving lives one person at a time, one day at a time. They help trans youth build resilience, gain confidence, and find hope for a future filled with joy. Founded in 2015 by a passionate mom, the organization continues to grow, serving an international population of families. standwithtrans.org

✳ <u>Stop Bullying</u>—StopBullying.gov provides information from various government agencies on what bullying is, what cyberbullying is, who is at risk, and how you can prevent and respond to bullying.
  ○ **LGBTQ+ Youth** https://www.stopbullying.gov /bullying/lgbtq

* Strong Family Alliance—Strong Family Alliance is an organization with a simple mission—to save lives and preserve families by helping children come out and parents become informed supporters and allies. https://www.strongfamilyalliance.org/
* Substance Abuse and Mental Health Services Administration (SAMHSA)—SAMHSA is the agency within the US Department of Health and Human Services that leads public health efforts to advance the behavioral health of the nation.
  ○ **A Practitioner's Resource Guide: Helping Families to Support Their LGBT Children** https://store.samhsa.gov/product/A-Practitioner-s-Resource-Guide-Helping-Families-to-Support-Their-LGBT-Children/PEP14-LGBTKIDS
* National Center for Trans Equality (NCTE)—NCTE was founded in 2003 by transgender activists who recognized the urgent need for policy change to advance transgender equality. With a committed board of directors, a volunteer staff of one, and donated office space, they set out to accomplish what no one had yet done: provide a powerful transgender advocacy presence in Washington, DC. https://transequality.org/
* Trans Families—Trans Families is a nonprofit organization that has been supporting transgender people and their families since 2008. Formerly called Gender Diversity, they are also the force behind the annual conference Gender Odyssey. https://transfamilies.org/
* Trans Language Primer—A guide to the language of gender, attraction, and acceptance. https://translanguageprimer.com/

✳ <u>Trans Lifeline</u>—Trans Lifeline is a grassroots hotline and microgrants 501(c)(3) nonprofit organization offering direct emotional and financial support to trans people in crisis—for the trans community, by the trans community. https://translifeline.org/

✳ <u>TransFamily Support Services</u>—TransFamily Support Services guide transgender/non-binary youth and their families through the gender transitioning process to help make it the most positive experience possible. They provide family coaching, assistance with healthcare and insurance issues, help navigating the legal system, and support at schools. All services are provided at no fee. https://www.transfamilysos.org

✳ <u>Transgender Law Center</u>—The Transgender Law Center employs community-focused strategies to ensure transgender individuals can thrive no matter where they live. Members advocate for equal treatment of transgender individuals in prisons, schools, healthcare facilities, and workplaces, helping to prevent discrimination and give members of the transgender community more freedom. https://transgenderlawcenter.org/

✳ <u>*Transforming* (Book by Austen Hartke)</u>—*Transforming* weaves ancient and modern stories that will change the way readers think about gender, the Bible, and faith.

✳ <u>Transition Forward Project</u>—Workplace assessment and resources for employers. https://transitionforward.org/resources/

✳ <u>Transmission Ministry Collective</u>—An online community dedicated to the spiritual care, faith formation, and leadership potential of transgender and gender-expansive Christians. https://transmissionministry.com

* ✳ The Reformation Project—The Reformation Project's mission is to advance LGBTQ+ inclusion in the church. https://reformationproject.org/
* ✳ The Trevor Project—The Trevor Project offers a variety of life-affirming programs to prevent suicide among LGBTQ+ individuals under the age of twenty-five. Trained counselors are available via telephone, text message, and instant message to provide crisis intervention when needed. The Trevor Project also offers training for teachers and other allies. *https://thetrevorproject.org
  * ○ **2023 US National Survey on the Mental Health of LGBTQ+ Young People** https://www.thetrevor project.org/survey-2023/
* ✳ Time to Thrive—National conference to promote safety for LGBTQ+ youths. https://timetothrive.org/
* ✳ *Unashamed: A Coming-Out Guide for LGBTQ Christians* (Book by Amber Cantorna)—*Unashamed* encourages LGBTQ+ Christians to embrace their unique identities and to celebrate the diversity placed inside them by God.
* ✳ US Department of Education—Laws, information, and resources surrounding education in the United States.
  * ○ **Resources for LGBTQ+ Students** https://www2 .ed.gov/about/offices/list/ocr/lgbt.html

Counseling and Crisis Resources

988 National Suicide and Crisis Lifeline—The 988 Suicide and Crisis Lifeline is a US-based suicide prevention network of over two hundred crisis centers that provides 24/7 service via a toll-free hotline with the number 9-8-8. It is available to anyone in suicidal crisis or emotional distress.

Association of LGBTQ+ Psychiatrists (AGLP)—Members are psychiatrists committed to conducting research to determine best practices in delivering mental health care to members of the LGBTQ+ community. Members also work with the American Psychological Association to influence policy and ensure that LGBTQ+ individuals can live their lives as free from discrimination as possible. http://www.aglp.org/

COLAGE—COLAGE is a resource for youth who have LGBTQ+ parents and stands as the only national organization dedicated to the empowerment of youth in LGBTQ+ families, and celebrates thirty years of this work. https://colage.org/connect/

LBGTQ Senior Hotline—Free and confidential peer support for the LGBTQ+ and questioning community ages fifty and above. Call 1-888-234-7242.

National Child Abuse Hotline—1-800-4AChild (1-800-422-4453) or text 1-800-422-4453.

National Domestic Violence Hotline—800-799-7233 or text LOVEIS to 22522.

National Sexual Assault Hotline—1-800-656-HOPE (4673) or online chat.

Open Path Collective—Open Path Psychotherapy Collective is a nonprofit nationwide network of mental health professionals dedicated to providing in-office and online mental health care—at a steeply reduced rate—to clients in need. https://openpathcollective.org/

Talk Space—Take a brief assessment, get matched with a provider, and start your journey. https://www.talkspace.com/

TimelyCare (for college students)—Great healthcare starts with high-quality mental health and medical care providers. TimelyCare's network of student-focused, culturally competent providers is working to improve campus health at colleges and universities across the country through evidence-based care that is effective, timely, and relevant to the campus community. https://timelycare.com/

The Trevor Project—Call: 1-866-488-7386; text: 678-678; or chat.

THRIVE—Thriving Harnesses Respect, Inclusion, and Vested Empathy: A crisis text line staffed by people in STEMM with marginalized identities. Text: 1-313-662-8209. https://thrivelifeline .org/

Trans Lifeline—1-877-565-8860 (*para Español, presiona el 2*).

ACKNOWLEDGMENTS

This book would not have been possible if not for those who have walked our journey with us and continue to love us well. Thank you to our dear friends Emily H., Keri and Aaron T., Jen S., Anna K., and Erin S., who have lovingly supported both our personal growth and our writing journey. We are so grateful for your presence in our lives.

A special thank-you to those who contributed their stories and insights to this book: Kassie, Sami, Kristin, Laura (and Matt too), and Jen M. Your words have added depth and insight for those who are walking this road with their loved ones.

A special thanks to Tree for being a thought partner and a true friend as we journey together and to Kristin for being the symbiotic friend whom Nia didn't know she so badly needed and for loving us so fiercely that we now will accept nothing less.

We would especially like to acknowledge Sami for her fierce and steady love for us and our family. We are so grateful for the endless support, advocacy, and encouragement you have given to us. We love you.

Thank you also to the Broadleaf team, particularly Lil Copan for taking a chance on our story and believing in a tiny seed of an idea. Finally, thank you, Lisa Kloskin, for helping us hone our words and for encouraging our voices.

Thank you all for shaping us, loving us, and embracing us.

NOTES

Introduction

1 If the use of the word *Queer* is uncomfortable for you, know that we will discuss in chapter 2 why we use the term.

Chapter 1

1 Susan Silk and Barry Goldman, "Ring Theory: How Not to Say the Wrong Thing," *Los Angeles Times*, April 7, 2013, www. latimes.com/opinion/op-ed/la-xpm-2013-apr-07-la-oe-0407-silk-ring-theory-20130407-story.html, accessed April 27, 2023.

2 Brené Brown, *Dare to Lead: Brave Work. Tough Conversations. Whole Hearts* (New York, NY: Random House Publishing Group, 2018), 22–23.

Chapter 3

1 Brené Brown, "*We Need to Talk about Shame,*" YouTube, August 10, 2022, https://www.youtube.com/watch?v=5C6UELitWkw&t=5s, accessed February 9, 2023.

2 The quote *"love the sinner, hate the sin"* is most often used in Evangelical Christian circles to denote that we ought to love everyone, although we are allowed to hate things about people that can be deemed as "sin." This is an impossible task as Queer identity, which is often labeled as the sin, is also part of the person who is being labeled as the sinner; thus, they are one and the same. It is our identity, not our ideology. For those who continue to use this language to talk

215

about how we can love Queer people while still hating some part of them, you must understand that this language is very damaging, essentially throwing the metaphorical sinner out with the sin. While we would encourage people to not use the word *sin* at all in the context of Queer identity, we hope people can stop using this phrase in particular as it is very damaging to Queer people of faith.

3 "2022 National Survey on LGBTQ Youth Mental Health," The Trevor Project, 2022, https://www.thetrevorproject.org/survey-2022/, accessed February 9, 2023.

4 The Centers for Disease Control (CDC) has a page of useful resources as well at https://www.cdc.gov/mentalhealth/tools-resources/individuals/index.htm, accessed June 20, 2023.

5 D. A. Rajah, *"Gayish: What Is Queer Joy and How Do I Get Some?"* Queer Insider, June 30, 2022, https://queerinsider.com/columns/gayish/gayish-what-is-queer-joy-and-how-do-i-get-some/, accessed February 9, 2023.

6 *Heartstopper* is a coming-of-age series on Netflix based on the best-selling graphic novels by Alice Oseman. It follows teens Nick and Charlie, who form an unlikely friendship and discover that it might be something more as they navigate school, love, and life.

7 B. Marling and Z. Batmanglij (writers), *Homecoming*, season one, episode one, December 16, 2016 [TV series episode]; *The OA*, Plan B Productions and Anonymous Content (original work published 2016).

Chapter 4

1 Brown, *Dare to Lead*, 48.

Chapter 5

1 Robert Pear, "'Transgender' Could Be Defined Out of Existence under Trump Administration," *New York Times*, October 21, 2018, https://www.nytimes.com/2018/10/21/us/politics/transgender-trump-administration-sex-definition.html, accessed March 22, 2023.

2 Semler (musician) in discussion with the authors, March 14, 2023.

3 The metaphor of metamorphosis, while apt, doesn't completely work here as the journey to identity doesn't always have a clear or final destination.

Chapter 6

1 National Suicide and Crisis Lifeline, dial 988.

2 National Abuse Hotline, 800-799-7233.

3 Gloria Willcox, "The Feeling Wheel," *Transactional Analysis Journal* 12, no. 4 (1982): 274–276, https://doi.org/10.1177/036215378201200411.

4 P. Boss, *Ambiguous Loss* (Cambridge, MA: Harvard University Press, 2000).

Chapter 7

1 Prentis Hemphill, *"A Reminder. Boundaries Are the Distance at Which I Can Love You and Me Simultaneously,"* Instagram, April 5, 2021, https://www.instagram.com/p/CNSzFO1A21C/?hl=en, accessed February 9, 2023.

Chapter 8

1 D. L. Moore, *No Ashes in the Fire: Coming of Age Black and Free in America* (New York, NY: Bold Type Books, 2019).

Chapter 9

1 A. Walker, *We Are the Ones We Have Been Waiting For: Inner Light in a Time of Darkness* (New York, NY: The New Press, 2007).

2 Elizabeth Myer, "The Best Part of Life by Glennon Doyle Melton," *SALT Project*, January 8, 2016, https://www.saltproject. org/progressive-christian-blog/2016/1/8/the-best-part-of-life-by -glennon-doyle-melton, accessed May 11, 2023.

NOTES

3 New International Version® (NIV®) Holy Bible, copyright © 1973, 1978, 1984, 2011 by Biblica, Inc.

4 NAS Exhaustive Concordance of the Bible with Hebrew-Aramaic and Greek Dictionaries, copyright © 1981, 1998 by the Lockman Foundation.

5 Martin Luther King Jr., Handwritten note. Auctioned by Moments in Time, https://abc7ny.com/mlk-day-martin-luther-king-junior-jr /5917393.

6 Alok Vaid-Menon, "Your Wound, My Garden" in *Your Wound, My Garden* (Self-Published, 2021), 48.

7 Alok Vaid-Menon, "Care Is Our Natural State" in *Your Wound, My Garden* (Self-Published, 2021), 51.

8 "Making Sanctuary: Hope, Companionship, Race and Emergence in the Anthropocene," *Bayo Akomolafe*, March 15, 2019, bayoakomolafe .net, accessed March 21, 2023.

Chapter 10

1 To learn more about the impact of figs on the environment, we recommend the book by Mike Shanahan, *God's Wasps and Stranglers: The Secret History and Redemptive Future of Fig Trees* (White River Junction, VT: Chelsea Green Publishing, 2016).

2 Erin Sanzero (friend) in conversation with the author, March 29, 2023.

3 Mary Daly, *Beyond God the Father: Toward a Philosophy of Women's Liberation* (Boston: Beacon Press, 1993).

4 Audre Lorde, "The Master's Tools Will Never Dismantle the Master's House" (1984) in *Sister Outsider: Essays and Speeches*, ed. Nancy K. Boreano (Berkeley: Crossing Press, 2007), 112.

5 Octavia E. Butler, "'There's Nothing New / Under the Sun, / But There Are New Suns': Recovering Octavia E. Butler's Lost Parables," Los Angeles Review of Books. June 9, 2014, https://lareviewofbooks .org/article/theres-nothing-new-sun-new-suns-recovering-octavia-e -butlers-lost-parables/, accessed July 12, 2023.

Toolkit

1 Maya Angelou, *I Know Why the Caged Bird Sings* (New York, NY: *Random House*, 1969).
2 "Neil DeGrasse Tyson Applied Science to the Tooth Fairy," YouTube, uploaded by *The Late Show with James Corden*, September 15, 2016, www.youtube.com/watch?v=BsR6sIsoWgU, accessed June 20, 2023.